Lifting

Lifting

Becoming the World's
STRONGEST BROTHERS

Tom and Luke
STOLTMAN

EBURY
SPOTLIGHT

Ebury Spotlight, an imprint of Ebury Publishing
20 Vauxhall Bridge Road
London SW1V 2SA

Ebury Spotlight is part of the Penguin Random House group of companies
whose addresses can be found at global.penguinrandomhouse.com

Penguin
Random House
UK

First published by Ebury Spotlight in 2023

www.penguin.co.uk

A CIP catalogue record for this book is available from the British Library

ISBN 9781529914412

Printed and bound in Great Britain by Clays Ltd, Elcograf S.p A.

Imported into the EEA by Penguin Random House Ireland,
Morrison Chambers, 32 Nassau Street, Dublin D02 YH68

FSC
www.fsc.org
MIX
Paper | Supporting
responsible forestry
FSC® C018179

Penguin Random House is committed to a sustainable future
for our business, our readers and our planet. This book is
made from Forest Stewardship Council® certified paper.

For Mum x

Contents

Prologue

If someone had told us years ago that, one day, we would be writing a book and sharing our story together, we would probably have burst out laughing.

It was definitely never part of any plan, that's for sure. Growing up in Invergordon, the small Scottish Highland town that we've always called home, the idea of becoming published authors was fairly low on our list of priorities. Besides, we've had various challenges to confront since then; Tom has been learning how to contend with autism, and there was the devastating loss of our Mum in 2016, too.

But this book has provided an opportunity to celebrate the things that mean the most to us, and we couldn't pass that up. Family, community, strength – both physical and mental – as well as humility and hard work, have always been our greatest focuses in life. The Stoltman story has been one of overcoming adversity and achieving your goals, even if they initially seem impossible. In writing this book, we hope to show that, whoever you are and wherever you come from, with the right attitude, you can handle anything that comes your way.

We hope you enjoy it.

Luke and Tom

1

ROLE MODEL

LUKE

There's an old photo of our Granddad Stoltman – or 'Opa', as his grandkids called him – carrying a huge log on his shoulder. He's bald, must be pushing 60, but he's not just carrying this log, he's running with it, with a big smile on his face. I've carried a few logs in my time – I've even tossed one or two – and I can tell you it's no picnic. But Opa's life was no picnic. Far from it.

Opa didn't talk much about his experiences in World War II, but he did write a book about them. And what a story it is. When Poland was invaded by German forces in September 1939, Opa's peaceful life turned into a living hell, literally overnight. His village was close to the German border, so it was quickly overrun. On day one of the occupation, Opa narrowly escaped a firing squad. You'd think things couldn't get much worse. Unfortunately, they did.

Some of Opa's neighbours were ethnic Germans, who threw their lot in with the invaders. Even some Poles switched sides. That meant Opa and his family had to be tough as old boots to survive, as well as very clever and resourceful.

Opa, still a teenager during the war, was put to work on German-owned farms. One of them was right next to a concentration camp, where he witnessed skeletal inmates being worked to death. At least he wasn't on that side of the fence.

Strange as it sounds, Opa was luckier than many of his neighbours. Some were evicted from their land. Others were beaten, murdered or simply disappeared. Meanwhile, the Stoltman family survived on their wits. Opa's dad owned a shop, so the Stoltmans were able to bribe Nazi officials and keep German neighbours – as well as traitorous Poles – onside. But it wasn't just sly stuff that kept them going. As Opa often said, 'The harder you work, the luckier you get.' And Opa slogged his guts out to keep himself and his family alive.

During the Nazi occupation, Opa stole kegs of whisky, slaughtered and butchered pigs, chopped wood, harvested crops, lugged grain, milked cows, drove posts and spread manure. The sort of stuff that will make you brutally strong. And through it all, he remained loyal to Poland and kept his dignity.

Opa did everything he could to postpone being drafted into the German army, including trying to poison himself with vinegar and cigarette butts. But he was only delaying the inevitable. Plus, if he'd dodged the draft, his family might well have been sent to a concentration camp. What the Germans didn't know was that Opa, patriot that he was, had already been sworn into a Polish resistance unit.

One time, Opa was with a bunch of German soldiers when some British bombers flew overhead. Instead of ducking for cover, he stood up and shouted, 'Over here! Over here!' If it meant German soldiers dying, he was prepared to take the risk. But Opa only hated the invaders in a general sense. He understood that not all Germans were evil. In fact, Opa made friends with quite a few ordinary Germans. If someone treated him well, he recognised that goodness.

The Nazis had invaded his homeland, displaced and killed millions, but Opa's spirit was never doused. Actually, some of my favourite Opa stories involve his little victories while in the German army. He disobeyed orders. He sweetened officers with wine and rabbits. He stole food and shared it with his mates. He used his uniform as cover to allow him to visit his brother, a priest in hiding. When he was sentenced to three months in a military prison, he thought about punching a guard, so he'd get another six months. When a German officer spoke of Opa 'fighting for the Fatherland' – meaning Germany – Opa gave him a piece of his mind. That could have got him shot. Instead, he was drilled so hard he considered killing himself. But Opa had the final say, eventually blackmailing the officer and getting preferential treatment. Opa must have had balls of steel.

After deserting the retreating German army, Opa ended up in an American prisoner-of-war camp in Belgium. And in January 1945, he joined up with the Polish army in the Scottish Highlands. The Polish war memorial that the soldiers built in Invergordon, using stone they found on a nearby beach, is still there. Meanwhile, the Russians had rolled into Poland. They were meant to be liberators, but in reality Opa's family had swapped one group of oppressors for another.

While in barracks, Opa discovered that his fiancée and brother had been killed in the closing stages of the war. When his mum didn't ask him to come home, he knew things must be seriously grim under Communist rule.

Opa didn't have enough money to return home anyway. So, when he was demobilised, he found himself stuck in a strange land, far from his beloved country and family. He had a choice: let despair overwhelm him or carry on fighting. Opa chose the latter, jumping on a bike with all his worldly goods and pedalling into the unknown. One of the first people he came across was an old tramp. Opa got his coins mixed up and accidentally gave him £3, a decent amount in those days. But Opa didn't mind. The future could only be brighter.

Opa knew almost no-one and didn't speak much English. But before long, he had a reputation as the hardest grafter for miles around. In fact, he grafted so hard that his fellow workers were suspicious of him, because he made them look like slackers. But the farm owners thought he was magnificent and spread the word: 'I've got this Polish lad, he'll tackle anything you throw at him and works like no-one else on earth. If you want anything doing, get him in.'

At Opa's funeral, farmers from all over the Highlands shared stories about him. They described how Opa would cycle 15 miles through snow and slush to dig their drains by hand; how he'd chop wood from dawn until dusk; how he was the greatest peat cutter they ever saw. They reckoned Opa was so tough, most modern men wouldn't be able to comprehend it.

Cutting peat sounds like a horrendous job, but back then, if you were good at it, it gave you a decent living. So Opa's fellow workers eventually stopped saying, 'That silly Polish boy works too hard.' Instead, the best of them were lining up to work on his squads. They were some of the hardest drinkers and dirtiest fighters in the Highlands, a real rum bunch, but they had so much respect for Opa. Even after he landed a big contract with a local distillery, to cut 12,000 cubic yards of peat a year, he continued to work alongside them. And he was so strong and so smooth, no-one came close to beating him.

Opa wasn't a particularly big man, like Tom and I are (he was just under 6ft tall, the smallest of his seven or eight brothers, one of whom was 6ft 7in), but doing that type of back-breaking work day after day for decades will make you strong as an ox – and almost immune to pain, yours or anyone else's.

When our dad joined one of Opa's squads, his hands were full of blisters after a couple of days. Opa couldn't care less. When our dad crushed his finger – he's still got the scars 50 years later – Opa looked at it and said, 'Oh … Go to doctor. You get lift on road.' Dad was in agony but did as he was told, because that was just Opa. When Opa arrived home later that night, he got it in the neck from Granny Stoltman. But he still couldn't see what the fuss was about. Given all the terrible things he'd experienced back in Poland, it's hardly surprising that a handful of blisters or a burst finger seemed like small beer.

Opa met Granny Stoltman – or Oma – in Invergordon, the town Tom and I still call home today. Opa had a wee cottage in nearby Alness, while Oma worked for a German woman who lived in the same village. In case you were wondering, Oma was German as well, but had been in Scotland since before the war.

They sound like an unlikely couple. But because Opa spoke more or less fluent German – and Oma was a bonny young woman – they clicked. When Opa wrote home to tell his parents he'd married a German, they disowned him. The Nazis had destroyed their country and killed one of his brothers, so in their eyes, it was one of the worst things he could have done.

Opa finally returned to Poland in 1959, a year after his dad died. That's when he learned exactly how bleak things had been. Shortly after the Russians turned up in their village of Powalki, Opa's parents were forced to close their shop, because private businesses run for profit weren't allowed. Opa's dad retired, and his mum found a job as a matron in a hospital. They were very poor, and life was a constant struggle, even for people as hardy as them. Opa's brothers and sisters were always asking, 'When will we be free again?'

When our dad visited in the early sixties, he was served soup that looked and tasted like milky water. He also remembers his aunties and uncles chewing on chicken feet. Opa would always comment on what a great life they had, and never mentioned that he was doing well in Scotland. But he felt so sorry for his brothers and sisters and was always sending them money. That's one of the reasons Opa grafted so hard: because he was doing it for all of them.

Opa had a soft side and loved playing with his grandkids. Saying that, he and Oma never stopped being formidable. While most of my friends' grandparents were small and fragile, they were sturdy and strong. They had to be, because they never stopped living off the land.

Having become an expert during the war, because he had to, Opa slaughtered and butchered his own pigs. And when I was a kid, me, my dad and Opa would go hunting together. We'd gut the deer where it fell, removing the innards and whatnot, pretty gory stuff. And whatever Opa shot – rabbit, hare, pigeon, pheasant or venison – ended up on the dinner table that evening.

When we visited our grandparents' house, where they grew their own vegetables, we'd weed the garden and dig up tatties. And when we weren't being put to work, we'd spend most of our time in the woods – riding our bikes, cutting down trees, building dens, making fires and jumping in rivers. That's probably why I enjoy jumping in cold water now, because it reminds me of being a kid. Sometimes we'd camp out all night, without telling our parents. When we finally came home, we'd be covered in scrapes and bruises. Us Stoltman kids certainly weren't wrapped in cotton wool – and we weren't cooped up in our bedrooms playing computer games. We were wild and free, and used to hard graft, and aches and pains, from an early age. As a result, we were getting strong, physically and mentally, without even knowing it.

Opa never stopped being a proud Polish man. I remember visiting our grandparents' house on Christmas Eve and tucking into Polish sausages and mustard, cucumber salad, mashed potato and dumplings. Opa also became a proud Highlander – and had the wonky accent to prove it. It was hugely important to him that our dad had sons to carry on the Stoltman name.

Opa had to do what he did to survive, which is very different from being a sportsman. But like Opa, Tom and I push ourselves to the limit every time we train and compete. Like Opa, we have the willpower to keep going when most people would quit. Without Opa, we wouldn't have achieved what we've achieved. He was an incredible man and stronger than we could ever imagine.

• • •

You won't be surprised to learn I was a big baby, over 10lbs. Poor Mum. Dad tells me that when I came out, I looked like a weird, wrinkly old Russian. Then the nurses took me next door and got my breathing going and some colour into me. It was a Thursday evening, about 7.50pm. Dad remembers *Top of the Pops* being on the telly and the nurses having to turn Shakin' Stevens down.

Dad worked offshore, as a surveyor in the oil and gas industries. It was decent money, but he spent a lot of time abroad. He'd be sent to all corners of the world at the drop of a hat, and we never knew when he'd be back. One job, he was supposed to be in South Korea for three weeks and ended up staying for six. When you're offshore, thousands of miles from home, it's not like you can do a swap with anyone, so it meant he missed a lot of birthdays and weddings.

Another time, Dad thought he was doing a quick hit in Cape Town and got stuck there for three months. While he was there, he worked seven days a week, sometimes late into the night. It was probably illegal, but a very good earner.

When I was four or five, Dad took the family with him to South Africa, where he was contracted to work for a year.

Unbeknown to them, Mum was pregnant. When the time came, she didn't fancy having a baby in Johannesburg, so she took me and my sister Jodie, their second child, back to Scotland. But because Dad couldn't break his contract, he didn't see the new baby, my sister Nikki, for three or four months.

Despite Dad's long absences, we still managed to have plenty of good times as a family. When I was born, Mum and Dad had a one-bedroomed flat. But a couple of years later, they cleared an area in the wilderness and built a wee wooden house. There was no road leading up to it and it was surrounded by nettles and lupins. Like Opa and Oma, Mum and Dad lived off the land. And because Mum couldn't drive, she'd cycle to the shops with me and Jodie in baskets, front and rear. Life was basic and uncomplicated, but there's a lot to be said for that. We were happy, which is all that really matters in life.

Dad's sisters kept having daughters, so for ten years I was the only boy in the family. A bit of a golden child. But when Mum had Tom and Harry in quick succession, the attention shifted to them. Dad was still away a lot, and Mum had her hands full with two babies, so I started acting up, seeing what I could get away with. To use Dad's words, I turned into a bit of a loon. As for Opa, he must have been horrified at some of the stuff I got up to as a teenager.

I was good at sport – I ran and played golf, tennis, rugby and football to a decent level – but I couldn't be doing with school. And when I was 17, I got expelled. I'd already tried to leave once, but went back after a short stint studying mechanical engineering at college. Me and two friends built a website, which sounds quite impressive. Problem was, it was all doctored pictures of our teachers. If I remember rightly, we turned one of them into a turkey.

The pictures were bad enough, but there was also a message board, so other pupils could post comments. As you can imagine, they weren't very nice. When the headmaster read some of the comments back to me, I couldn't help laughing. To be fair, they were pretty funny. Eventually he lost his temper, told me to collect my belongings, leave the premises and never come back.

I was too young to join my dad offshore, so I ended up working in a supermarket and a fish factory. And when I wasn't knee deep in fish guts, I was getting up to no good. If you live in the Highlands, driving is a necessity. But 17-year-olds aren't interested in pootling to the shops and back. Instead, I'd race my mates, and the first ticket I got was for speeding. That meant a six-month ban. Then, just a few months after getting my licence back, I decided to drive home from the pub after quite a few too many. That didn't end well either.

Dad was in Azerbaijan, high up on some oil rig, when he got the call from Mum. The poor woman was beside herself. The police had found Dad's white van on the beach, on its roof with its wheels still spinning. But they couldn't find me. Dad said all the right things – 'What a silly bugger! Wait until I get home!' – but apparently he was trying not to laugh. Sounds strange, I know, but he was also a bit off the rails as a young man – liked a party, drank and smoked too much, unlike Mum – so he sensed I was probably okay.

After flipping the van, I'd hightailed it across the fields and gone to my girlfriend's house. I was lying on the couch, still blazing drunk, when the police turned up. I told them they didn't need to handcuff me, but when I stood up and they saw how big I was, they decided it was probably a good idea. I spent the night in the cells, until I'd sobered up, before being charged with drink-driving. I avoided a stretch in prison, but I did get another six-month ban.

• • •

Growing up in Invergordon, the rest of the world seemed a long way away. It's got beautiful surroundings, everybody knows each other and the pace is nice and slow – if you're sitting in traffic for a minute, that's a big deal. The one problem with Invergordon is that there aren't as many opportunities as in lots of other places. At school, no-one ever said to me, 'You can do anything you want.' Instead, careers officers would say, 'You can be a farmer, work in the distillery, work for the Forestry Commission or out on the rigs.' Mum and Dad were always positive, but I didn't dream big, because I didn't know anything big was out there.

It was a lot easier to get a start on the rigs in those days, and for my 18th birthday, Dad bought me an offshore survivor course. A week or so after doing that course, I paid my first visit to a rig. I hadn't been on a helicopter before and I was petrified. I didn't open my eyes from the time we took off to the time we landed. Then, on only my second day offshore, I phoned Mum and said, 'This is awful. I don't think it's for me.' I was almost in tears. But she replied, 'Well, you'll just have to stick it out because you can't come home.'

Life offshore was a rude awakening. Overnight, I'd gone from doing some rubbish job, partying every weekend with no responsibilities, to living in the middle of the sea, feeling like a spare part. I was totally green and didn't have a clue. But I soon started to learn the ropes and eventually settled into things.

I got a little bit of stick, partly because Dad had landed me the job, but mainly because I was so young and naive. Surveying was a bit niche, so I'd always be travelling to different rigs and meeting new people. But because I'd had a sheltered upbringing, out in the sticks, I was very shy and reserved. In stark contrast, the rigs were full of big, rough lads who'd been working offshore for years. Those early days were really quite intimidating.

The old hands would rib me for falling asleep in the tea shack because I was knackered. They'd scream in my face – 'Wake up, ya shite bag!' – and slap me around the head. They'd shout at me for taking a tape reading wrong. That happened quite a lot, because I didn't even know what a millimetre was. Nowadays, you'd probably call that bullying. Back then, they called it character building. And, to be fair to them, I needed to toughen up.

Working offshore is a bit like being in the military. While I was out there, I'd get my head down, work hard and not drink for a few weeks. Then I'd return to Invergordon and sit in the pub for five days straight. The money wasn't great when I started, something like £5 an hour, but it was enough to get smashed, because I wasn't spending any money while I was on the rigs.

A couple of days before I was due to go offshore again, I'd get quite down, because I knew what was coming – three more weeks of grinding work. Sometimes, we'd go down to Aberdeen the day before we were due to fly out, pile into a pub and drink as much as we could. I'd wake up in a strange house at 6am and have to be at the heliport at 7am. I'd be rough as anything on the helicopter, praying I wouldn't be breathalysed on arrival. Then the cycle would start all over again: head down, hard work, detoxing from the drink.

On my first trip to America, I got corrupted by a mate of my dad's, Brucie. That man loved a drink and made a complete mess of me, as I did of him. One time, I walked into the bar and Brucie ordered two bottles of champagne, one for me and one for him. When we'd drunk them – about five minutes after he'd bought them – Brucie roared, 'Right, now it's your round!' He was earning about five times more than me, but I couldn't really complain.

Brucie took off before I could give him his bottle, leaving me stranded. The following morning, he was nowhere to be seen. It transpired he'd gone to some party, woken up in a panic and hightailed it to the site, only to discover it was 3am. He had a short kip and was back at work at 7am.

We worked ludicrously long shifts – 14-hour days were quite normal. And the work could be stressful – it was always, 'When are you gonna finish this? Can you do this as well?' One time, I worked 60 days straight, 56 of them offshore. When the rig manager finally got round to looking at my hours, he went berserk – 'What the hell are you doing? You haven't had a day off for two months!' I was flown back to shore on the evening chopper, but ended up working in the office for the following few days before being flown back out to finish the job.

No wonder the blowouts were so messy. They almost had to be, for the sake of our sanity. And I fully expected to follow the same routine for the rest of my working life. Graft, blowout, graft, blowout, ad nauseam. What else was a kid with no qualifications from little old Invergordon expected to do?

2

CHILDHOOD CHALLENGES

TOM

Opa passed away when I was ten, so I don't remember much about him. But I do remember thinking, 'Jesus, how the heck is he my granddad? It's not right.' Whenever I walked into his house, he just seemed to loom over everything. It confused me, because granddads aren't supposed to be big and strong, they're supposed to be little old men who spend all day sat in an armchair.

When I look at that photo of Opa with a log on his shoulder, I think, 'That's not normal. Who picks up a log and goes for a wee run, just for the craic?' Luke and I do stuff like that now, but we're professional strongmen.

Even when Opa was on his last legs he seemed massive to me. Maybe the Polish are just made different. Then again, Oma's side of the family are even bigger than Opa's – most of our male cousins on the German side are well over 6ft. I remember visiting Oma in a care home, towards the end of her life, and being shocked at how tall she still was. I think about Opa and Oma now and everything makes perfect sense. Luke and I have worked very hard to get where we are, but we had seriously good genes, no doubt about that.

Sometimes, kids would ask where my family came from, but most people thought Stoltman was just an unusual Scottish name. I certainly didn't feel exotic growing up, although we were more multicultural than most families in Invergordon. Oma would mainly cook us German food, which I preferred to Polish stuff. I also loved going to the Christmas market in Inverness. There would be proper German sausages in those big hotdog rolls, German hams and wee biscuits that I really liked, like shortbread but with loads of sugar. I'd spend hours browsing the different stalls, my mouth watering, and eating as much as I could. Not that it made me fat. Actually, I was skinny as a rake.

I was diagnosed with autism when I was five or six, but not without a fight. Whenever Mum took me to see the specialist, I'd be on my best behaviour, probably because I was so shy. As a result, the specialist didn't think there was anything wrong with me. In the end, Mum was forced to record me having a tantrum. Only when the specialist saw the footage did he say, 'Oh, he's autistic.' I find that unbelievable. Why would he not believe someone who'd spent almost every waking hour with me since I was born?

Even after I was diagnosed with autism, I didn't understand it. I still thought my behaviour was normal and everyone else was acting different. To this day, I can't really explain how being autistic makes me feel compared to other people. But I do know my childhood could be very scary.

Despite that, I have fond memories of my time at Newmore Primary School. It was a wee school, with about 30 pupils.

I felt safe there, because I knew everyone and I knew exactly what was going to happen every day. Every break time, we'd play football. And when I had a football at my feet, I'd feel like a normal kid. I'd get home and kick a ball against a wall for hours. Or I'd get my wee brother Harry, who was only a year and a half younger than me, to go in goal. Football was a comfort for me, a distraction. When I played, I felt on top of the world. But when I didn't have my football, my autism would be there for all to see.

For example, I fought a lot with my sister Nikki, and when I wrestled with Harry, I'd take it far too seriously. Going to busy, noisy places really affected me. When Mum took me shopping, I'd start screaming in the supermarket. I had to be with Mum all the time, she couldn't leave the house without me. And if Harry or Jodie went out, I'd be phoning them every ten minutes to see where they were. I wasn't as attached to Luke, because he was ten years older than me. But if he was going offshore or away on holiday, he'd have to phone me when he arrived at his destination and every few hours after that, otherwise I'd kick off.

When you're an autistic child, most of the emphasis is on you, even when there are four other kids in the house. Luckily, I had understanding brothers and sisters, who never questioned why I was getting more attention from Mum and Dad. Harry always accompanied me to football training, and I assumed he loved the game like me. Later, I found out he hated football and only came along because I wouldn't go by myself. Wee Harry was more like an older brother and very protective. He did loads of stuff he wasn't into, but never resented it. As far as he was concerned, it was just the right thing to do.

Dad being away for long periods was hard for me to understand. I'd think, 'Why does he keep coming and going? Why doesn't he want to stay?' Looking after five kids on her own would have been tough enough for Mum, but I'd behave even worse when Dad was away. Certain things would trigger my tantrums. For example, if Mum told me to go to bed, I'd go berserk, lock myself in the bathroom and scream the house down. Eventually, Mum learned to modify her language, so my tantrums would only last three or four minutes, instead of an hour. But I never stopped making life difficult for her.

Dad would sometimes be away for months at a time. I remember Mum crying, because she was finding it so difficult. And it must have been hard for Dad as well. He missed big chunks of our childhoods, and he knew Mum was getting the worst of me. Not that Mum ever questioned Dad. He was going offshore before they had kids, so she knew what she was getting into. And when I got a bit older, she was able to explain why Dad did what he did: 'He's going away to earn money, so we can provide for you kids and make your lives better.' I understood it then, and it helped me calm down a wee bit.

While primary school was a walk in the park, things went downhill fast after I transferred to the academy. Primary school had been small and cosy, but secondary school was big and terrifying. Suddenly, I was in a class with 30 or so noisy, hyperactive kids. I had lots of different lessons in lots of different rooms. There were strange new rules and lots of choices. Should I get my lunch on the high street or from the canteen? That sort of stuff blew my mind. After a while, I avoided going whenever I could, because it was all too much for me.

Mum and Dad had a lot of hassle trying to get me the help I needed. When they tried to explain to a senior teacher that I just needed a bit of one-on-one support, to boost my confidence, he said that couldn't possibly happen. That really annoyed Dad, because as far as he was concerned, there was no such thing as 'can't'. He said to the teacher, 'If you *think* you can do something, you can!' He knew that for a fact, because of Opa's example.

Eventually, Mum and Dad got in touch with somebody at the education centre in nearby Dingwall, and explained that I was in danger of being lost in the school system. After that, I finally got some one-on-one help. Dad was right, a different approach was possible. But even with the extra help, life at the academy was a bit of a struggle.

The support teachers were great, but I found it a bit humiliating. The other kids wondered why I was getting one-on-one lessons in a different room, why I didn't do exams with them, why I didn't come in some days, why I got to go home before them. They didn't see how I behaved at home, behind closed doors, so they didn't know I was autistic. They just thought I was a normal kid.

Mum didn't want to baby me, so left it up to me to tell people about my autism. And when I was 14, I decided to tell seven or eight of my mates, because I was fed up being judged all the time. Other kids might have turned their backs on me, thought I was weird, but my friends stuck with me, accepted me for who I was. That was a big weight off my shoulders. Suddenly, I felt like a normal member of society. Yes, I was a bit different, but knowing my mates were going to treat me the same as anyone else was a great comfort.

I'd always been quite popular anyway, because I lived and breathed football. Dad was more into rugby than football, but Luke played a bit for Ross County, our local team, and I caught the bug from him. I used to go to County home games because I had mates who went. But my real passion was Glasgow Rangers. For ages, I could only watch them on TV, because Dad wasn't interested in taking me all the way to Glasgow. But he caved in the end. I can't remember who Rangers played in my first game at Ibrox, but I've been utterly obsessed with them ever since.

I was a tall, lanky teenager. I looked like a Scottish Peter Crouch – actually, I was probably skinnier than him. Unlike Crouchy, I played in defence, but I had plenty of skill, because I practised so much. Both Rangers and Ross County were interested in signing me up, mainly because of my size. But wearing glasses didn't help. Neither did my autism.

I really struggled with the travelling. If my local team, Invergordon FC, were playing a long way from home, Mum or Dad would have to come with me, otherwise I'd panic. Mum and Dad paid for me to go to Rangers camps, and I played for the county. But meeting and playing with different people stressed me out. I wouldn't say a word for the entire game, which coaches didn't look kindly on.

Whenever I met new people when I was out with Mum, my hood would be up, my head would be down, my legs would be shaking, my hands would be fidgeting, and I'd be staring at my shoes. I'd start stuttering and just about manage to say 'hi', but nothing more than that. If Mum bumped into someone she knew, she'd chat away for ages while I stood there like a mute.

I only started using public transport when I was 15, and only then with support workers. I started out doing wee journeys to my sister's house, or five-minute train rides. I found it terrifying and wore headphones so no-one would talk to me. But, after a while, I started taking train rides on my own. After my first solo train ride, one stop from Tain to Invergordon, we had a big celebration.

Through it all, Mum and Dad never gave up on me. It was always a case of, 'Tom's got autism, what's the big deal?' They were unbelievable parents. Dad sacrificed so much and taught us the virtue of hard work. And Mum was the most caring person in the world, totally committed to making sure everything was perfect for her kids. If it wasn't for Mum and Dad, I wouldn't be where I am now. I'd be sat in their house, a shy, stuttering man, drifting through life.

As Harry and my sisters got older, they were able to take more of the slack. Jodie, who is very similar to me, even went off and studied autism so she could understand me better. She'd take me to after-school activities for kids with different needs and started up her own clubs that ran during the school holidays. Jodie knew how I was feeling without me needing to say anything. That took a lot of pressure off Mum and helped me no end.

Unfortunately, it was still easy for other people to put me off my stride. I wanted to be a footballer well into my teens, couldn't think of anything else I could do. Then my PE teacher told me I'd never amount to anything, because I didn't work hard enough at the theory side of things. It must have been frustrating for that teacher. She probably saw potential in me and thought I was squandering it. And maybe she thought a few home truths would light a fire under me. But being an autistic kid, I took things very literally. If my teacher thought I'd never amount to anything, then she must be right.

That really knocked my confidence. If I was just going to sit at home, not doing the only thing that brought me comfort, I thought there was no point living. I locked myself in my bedroom for a few weeks and refused to go to school. Mum couldn't drag me there – I was already far too big for that.

That was a dark time, and I know Mum was very worried about me. But after a few weeks of playing computer games and stuffing myself with junk food, I thought, 'I want to prove that teacher wrong. I won't do it in class – my brain doesn't work that way. But I will find something. And in a few years' time, she'll look at me and say, "Wow. I was wrong about that boy …'

3

BIG BROTHER

LUKE

B eing ten years older than Tom, I was very aware that something was different about him from an early age. He wouldn't go to nursery some days, because he didn't want to leave Mum. And on the rare occasions Mum went to the shops on her own, leaving the other kids with Jodie and me, Tom would go into a frenzy, almost like a fit, and we wouldn't be able to calm him down.

We'd have to tell him we were going to phone Mum, to find out where she was. And if she came home even slightly later than she intended, he'd go off again. Tom can't remember some of this, probably because it was so traumatic. But I recall that when he had one of his tantrums, I'd pick him up, bounce him on my knee and distract him with a colourful toy parrot, which had wings attached to some strings. Or I'd get him to wrestle me, or take him outside for a kickabout. A game of football seemed to be the best medicine.

I didn't really know what autism was when I was a teenager, apart from having seen the film *Rain Man*. And Tom was nothing like the main character in that. But because he and Harry were so close in age, we were able to compare their progression. While Harry went to school without any problems, did his homework and interacted with people, Tom couldn't do any of that. He was very nervous and awkward around strangers, couldn't even look at them, never mind have a conversation. And he found any slight change of routine very difficult to deal with. Tom's world must have been a very scary place.

At primary school, if they did something different in class, he'd freak out and Mum would have to go and pick him up. He'd also go into a panic if he didn't know where I was. And he hated me getting drunk, which I did a lot in my teenage years. It altered my personality, which must have been a nightmare for Tom: one minute I was his cuddly big brother, wrestling and playing football with him, the next I was a noisy, slurring idiot. I was self-centred, like a lot of teenagers, and not really thinking about anyone else.

Mum always used to say, 'The word "can't" is just another way of sugar-coating excuses.' But I don't know how she coped. It was a constant battle for her. And things must have seemed very bleak when that PE teacher said what she did and Tom fell into a depression. Everyone knew Tom wasn't academic, but he did love sport. He must have felt like his world had fallen apart.

To my mind, the Scottish education system could be better at providing places for non-academic kids to discover their passions and learn skills to help them reach their full potential.

It's having the confidence to say, 'Right, this kid's no good at maths or physics, but that doesn't mean he's stupid. Maybe he's good with his hands?' Not everyone can be a doctor or a lawyer, but there are so many other things you can do.

Carpentry, plastering or fitting bathrooms might not sound like the sexiest jobs, but they are well-respected, involve a lot of skill and can earn you good money. Likewise, Tom should have been encouraged to pursue the one thing that made him happy, the one thing he excelled at: sport. Instead, those few misplaced words made him feel utterly worthless.

• • •

Because Mum had to focus on Tom, and Dad was away so much, I started acting up, probably because I was craving attention. That might also explain why I became so obsessed with working out in the gym.

I vividly remember my first visit to the gym, when I was 16. There was this massive guy in a little string vest, with a huge tattoo on his back. I thought, 'Jesus, that's absolute class. I wonder if I could get as big as him?' I was still very shy and reserved, so didn't go out much with my mates. But I immediately felt very comfortable in the gym. Some of the guys were shifting enormous weights, which sounds intimidating, but I was able to switch off from that. Soon, I was working out for four or five hours a day, doing hundreds of reps and getting bigger and bigger. I couldn't get enough of it.

The great thing about the gym is that it's easy to quantify your progression. If I did ten reps one week, I'd do 11 reps the following week, and know for a fact I was getting stronger. And before long, I was one of the strongest in the gym. When I bench-pressed 140kg, other blokes in the gym started showing an interest. I'd usually see them looking at me out of the corner of their eyes. I could also see my body changing, which made me feel great. To be honest, it was more about vanity than strength at the beginning.

I subscribed to *Flex*, a bodybuilding magazine that had photos of musclebound blokes posing in their pants. I'd go to the gym right before a night out so my biceps were as pumped as possible. When I was 18 or 19, I started getting compliments about my physique. I suppose it was a cover for my lack of confidence. By my early twenties, I was calling myself the strongest man in the North Sea and ripping my shirt off in the pub. It became an expensive habit, because it got to the stage where people were disappointed if I didn't.

Getting stronger and sculpting my body was by far the most important thing in my life – nothing else really mattered. When I was working in Aberdeen, I went to three different gyms a day, because I wanted to try out all the machines. And when I was working offshore, I'd improvise. Working in the oil industry you can find yourself in some pretty far-flung places. In Angola, where I regularly worked, the offshore gym was awful, hardly anything in it. So, I made weights from scaffold poles with sandbags attached to each end. Or I'd do pull-ups and dips on the iron beams that were scattered around the plant.

Whenever I was sent overseas to work offshore and checked into a hotel, the first question I would ask the receptionist was, 'Do you have a gym?' If they didn't, I'd have to go and find one. In Louisiana, where Dad's mate Brucie led me astray, I'd finish my shift, head back to the hotel, get a taxi to the gym and do a two-hour session, before meeting the boys in the bar.

By the time I turned up, they'd all be blazing drunk, but I'd soon catch up. Even when I was back in Invergordon, out with my friends every day, I'd always get up the following morning, make it to the gym and grind it out. If I got a session done, everything else seemed to be okay.

When I was 25, I entered a local deadlift competition. I was still more into bodybuilding, but thought to myself, 'If I'm dead-lifting over 300kg, I might as well give it a shot.' After winning that comp, I got chatting with the guy who finished second, a lad called Peter Macdonald-Brown. Peter was a city boy, but we immediately hit it off, and he suggested I give strongman a go.

I should probably take this opportunity to clear up a popular misconception. People assume my and Tom's route into strong-man was via Highland games, which is understandable. We are, after all, from the Highlands, and Highland games were, for many years, where Highlanders showed off their strength.

But Highland games requires a completely different skillset to strongman. A few strongmen have dabbled in the 'weight for height' event, which involves throwing a weight over a bar, but the rest of Highland games doesn't really cross over. Strongmen are bigger and stronger overall, but Highland games compet-itors are more athletic and technical. You're more likely to get Olympic athletes competing in Highland games – like Geoff Capes, who represented Great Britain in the shot put before winning World's Strongest Man twice – because they're already masters of some of the crafts.

On top of that, Highland games weren't really on my radar when I was growing up. When our dad was a kid, there was a

Highland games in Invergordon every August, with tug of war, hammer throwing, stone put and, of course, caber tossing. The best competitors were local celebrities, including a lad called Big Sandy, who lived in Ardross and died only recently. But over the years, the number of Highland games taking place has decreased.

In contrast, World's Strongest Man was on TV every Christmas, and it seemed a lot more modern and sexy. Not that I'd ever considered doing it before Peter piped up. Strongmen just seemed so exotic, and it was like they just appeared on your TV fully formed. I had no idea how you became one and couldn't see a connection between what I was doing in the gym and what they were doing, like pulling trucks and lifting cars. But Peter invited me to do some strongman training with him at Forge Gym in Inverness, and I was immediately hooked. I was still pushing my body to its limit, but in different ways. Plus, there was a more competitive element, which appealed to me.

I had a lot of respect for bodybuilders, and still do, but they have to be ridiculously strict with their diets. My job didn't allow that, because I couldn't control what I ate offshore. Besides, hardly eating for days on end didn't really appeal to me – bodybuilders have to follow a really regimented diet, some-times a very minimal diet to get into their desired weight class for competing. So, the whole strongman thing was starting to make sense, even if I didn't look like your classic strongman yet, with that rounder shape they have.

I was clearly unusually strong, but I also had the madness required. The vast majority of gym-heads wouldn't even consider becoming a strongman. They're quite happy just fiddling about on the machines. Then you'll get the people who dabble in strongman and think, 'This is a bit too weird for me.' Or they'll find it too daunting. I've seen behemoths, with muscles on top of muscles, who just don't fancy it. You'll see the fear in their eyes, because they're convinced they're going to do themselves a mischief. Or they'll run through the events – dumbbell pressing, lifting a 180kg sandbag onto their shoulder, doing a farmer's walk, lifting some stones – and they'll be dying. You just know you're never going to see them doing strongman again.

I was one of the few people who embraced that weirdness. I would sometimes think, 'This is insane – I've spent the last few hours in a cold, musty gym, lifting stones and getting covered in muck.' But after a good session, I'd be on cloud nine, because I knew I was stronger than 99.99 per cent of the world's population, or at least all the people not training for strongman. I'd think about lifting weights every minute of every day, and I'd look forward to the pain of being in the gym.

I wasn't just attracted to the glamour and fun of strongman, the competitions in exotic places you saw on TV. I also loved all the dirty stuff, the effort and the sacrifice needed to get there. Not even the danger factor bothered me. And I soon learned that the stronger and more technical you get, the less danger-ous strongman is. Pressing dumbbells can smart a bit, because it often catches your ear on the way past your head. But if you're unable to complete a lift, there's a way of ditching it without hurting yourself. Then again, I have seen plenty of people drop dumbbells on their heads. That must sting a bit. I'll be standing there thinking, 'Jesus, mate, it's a 100kg dumbbell, maybe think about jumping out of the way.'

Thankfully, the worst injury I've suffered is an crushed finger, when it got stuck between a 140kg stone and the platform. I didn't break any bones, but the cut and bruising were fairly bad. A couple of weeks later, I was doing the frame carry in Britain's Strongest Man, the weight came down on my finger and it burst open again. Not pleasant, but I've been pretty lucky compared to some.

I've seen rivals tear biceps, quads and pectorals, while one poor guy dropped an Atlas Stone – those massive spheres you see us loading onto platforms on World's Strongest Man – and snapped his shin bone clean in two. Then there was the time someone tossed a keg, it bounced off the crossbar, landed on his head and knocked him out. But that was a freak accident. Strongmen are like any other professional athletes. We practise hard to minimise mistakes, so just like you almost never see a pro golfer topping a ball, you'll almost never see a strongman dropping something on his toe.

A couple of months after I started strongman training, Peter and I competed in Highland's Strongest Man. It wasn't the most glamorous occasion – it took place in a gym car park – but I think I won every event, which was a bit of a surprise, and afterwards Peter suggested I enter Scotland's Strongest Man. I'd automatically qualified by winning Highland's Strongest Man, but my immediate reaction was, 'Don't think so, mate! There are millions of people in Scotland. I'll get taken to the cleaners by the city lads, completely humiliated!'

But after a bit of persuasion, I decided to give Scotland's Strongest Man a go. I was working on a project in Hamburg at the time, and the gym I found, which was just a bog-standard one, didn't have any strongman equipment. That wasn't really a surprise – you don't tend to see many Atlas Stones in Fitness First. I was due to fly back to Scotland on the Friday, to compete in Scotland's Strongest Man on the Saturday. But after my shift on the Thursday, I decided to head straight to the pub and get absolutely hammered.

I was still in the pub at 4am, when the barmaid said to me, 'You're an idiot! Your taxi's coming in half an hour, and you're competing tomorrow!' I told her I wasn't going, that the whole idea was stupid. My confidence had ebbed away, and I'd convinced myself that I was going to get it all wrong. But the barmaid wasn't having any of it. She closed the pub and kicked me out.

I just managed to catch the plane to Edinburgh, got a cab to Dumfries, arrived at my hotel and slept all the way through until 10am the following morning, a couple of hours before the competition was scheduled to start. I did manage to smash down some breakfast, but it was very far from ideal preparation.

I was the first competitor to arrive at the venue, which was nothing fancy, just a local gym. I spent half an hour sitting alone with my thoughts, absolutely bricking myself. Then the other guys started rocking up, and they were all massive. As I watched them file in, I was thinking, 'Blimey, I've seen him on TV. Oh God, I think that other bloke won it last year … Look at the size of him! What on earth am I doing here?' Meanwhile, they were probably all thinking, 'Who the hell is that guy? Where the hell has he popped up from?'

At least I had plenty of support, because Mum and Dad came down with a load of mates from Invergordon. I didn't talk to them, because I was so nervous. But I couldn't help hearing them. Whenever I did an event, Mum would scream like a banshee. And as the competition progressed, she got squeakier and squeakier, and louder and louder. I could see people looking confused, probably thinking, 'Who the hell is making all that racket?' But that was our mum, a woman who supported her kids with everything she had.

Not even Mum thought I had a chance of winning the thing. She and Dad thought I was just a gym-head who was doing this competition for a laugh. I'd never even lifted an Atlas Stone or done a log press before that day. Peter had a Swiss bar in his gym, which is a barbell with a square section in the middle, but it wasn't quite the same. On top of that, his dumbbells only went up to 60kg, and I knew the best could press over 100kg.

But, to everyone's surprise, including mine, I kept winning events. And suddenly the other guys started talking to me, asking where I was from and telling me how strong I was. That was nice, boosted my confidence and made me feel even stronger.

Before the Atlas Stones, which was the final event, two lads in front of Mum and Dad started talking about me. One said, 'He must be Scandinavian with that name, so won't qualify for Britain's Strongest Man if he wins.' How they hadn't noticed Mum's shrill Highland tones before then is anyone's guess.

As it turned out, I won the stones, and the competition, before ripping my shirt off and screaming, 'This is easy!' It hadn't been, but I had this intuition that I needed to put on a bit of a show. I even had a nickname already, 'The Highland Oak'. My friends from the gym had come up with it; they knew Arnold Schwarzenegger (a.k.a. the Austrian Oak) was an idol of mine, and we found the play on words funny. Before that day, strongman in Scotland had been getting a bit stagnant. But a big storm had blown in from the Highlands, sweeping away the field and shaking up the sport.

And there was a new storm on its way – even bigger than me.

4

LIFTING WEIGHTS AND FINDING MY ROCK

TOM

W hen I was growing up, there was a Rangers support-
ers' club near us. Glasgow is a four-hour bus journey
from Invergordon, and the club organised trips so Highland
fans could watch the matches in person. When I was 16, Dad
bought me a season ticket and I started following them obses-
sively. Strangely, the big crowds at Ibrox didn't bother me.
That's maybe because I was just one of thousands, and there
was no attention on me. In fact, I loved the noise, and I loved
making it. I could shout as loud as I liked, sing all the songs and
enjoy being a normal human being.

Unfortunately, Rangers went into liquidation in 2012, and
the reformed club had to start down in the Third Division. That
was pretty devastating. But it made me feel like a proper football
fan who supports their team through thick and thin, instead of
just when they're winning things. I watched Rangers every week
when they were in the Third Division, playing teams like East
Stirlingshire, Elgin and Berwick. The bus journey to Annan, down
on the border with England, took five or six hours. We drew 0-0.

While Rangers were making their way back up through the
divisions, Celtic were winning trophy after trophy. That could

be painful, because Celtic are our bitter rivals. But I loved those years, wouldn't swap them for anything. When you've experienced the lows as a football fan, it makes the highs even sweeter. When Rangers were promoted back to the Scottish Premiership in 2016, it was one of the best moments of my life.

I never did fulfil my dream of playing for Rangers at Ibrox. When most of my friends hung up their boots, I thought, 'Well, that's my football career over', because I didn't want to play with anyone else. Because of my autism, I found playing with strangers a bit of an ordeal. I left school with not a lot of qualifications, before enrolling on a personal fitness sports course. I dropped out after a year, because I didn't see the point and I didn't enjoy it. I then studied forestry with Harry in Inverness, but I wasn't destined to be a forester either. I didn't have a clue what I wanted to do, and nobody had high hopes for me. But then, when I was 16, Luke persuaded me to go to the gym with him. He thought I might fall in love with shifting weights, just like he had.

At that time, around 2010, I was really lost. I thought I might never leave Mum and Dad's house. And the gym didn't seem like a way out, not in the early days. That first time, I stuck to Luke like a limpet. As usual, I had my hood up and my head down. When Luke introduced me to one of his mates, I mumbled 'hi' and stared at my shoes. To be honest, I hated every minute of it, like I hated anything new.

When you're autistic, three of the worst things are crowds, mirrors and people watching you. So, a busy gym was my worst nightmare, because it's always bustling and there are mirrors everywhere. Luke was telling me to lift this and lift that, and I just felt mortified. I was this lanky kid with glasses, surrounded by beautiful people. Luke looked good, his mates looked good, the girls looked good, and everyone was stronger than me. I couldn't even lift the bar on its own. I remember thinking, 'This might be Luke's thing, but it's really not my cup of tea. Get me back on a football pitch, anything but this.'

The following morning, I was sore all over. I was used to getting lumps and bumps playing football, but this was on a whole different level. I could barely move, struggled to tie my shoelaces. And the logical part of my brain was saying, 'How is this supposed to be enjoyable? And even if I'm good at it, I don't want to lift dumbbells and pose in front of the mirror for the rest of my life.'

I usually quit when things got hard. I quit school, I quit college, I quit football. But not this time, because I had Luke as a protective cloak. I didn't have to ask random people how to use the machines. Instead, I'd just follow Luke around and do whatever he told me to do. Luke also explained that most people feel self-conscious when they start going to the gym, and that no-one cared what I looked like or how much I was lifting.

Luke was desperate for me to make something of myself, so he kept on at me. He could have easily said, 'If you fancy coming to the gym once or twice a week, that's cool.' But he made sure I was there with him every day. He was even telling me what to eat. From not being particularly close, we were suddenly almost inseparable. And if it wasn't for him, I don't know where I'd be today.

Luke kept everything very simple while teaching me proper technique. When I started out in the gym, I thought you just walked up to something and lifted it, however you could. But Luke said to me, 'Don't focus on the weight. Focus on the form and the weight will follow.' That's why I progressed so fast and never got injured, because I had the fundamentals down to a T. While my mates were hitting a ceiling, because their techniques weren't right and they were picking up niggles, I was crashing through it. Although still skinny at this stage, I was taller than most of my friends and brute strength was important, no doubt about that. But my form was the key to everything.

Luke told his mates I was autistic, so they went out of their way to be welcoming. I was still very shy and reserved, but the gym began to feel like a safe place. After a couple of weeks, I was able to have conversations with some of them. And when Luke went back offshore, I felt confident enough to go without him. Mum would drop me off and pick me up, and Harry started coming along as well. That made things even more comfortable.

When Luke returned from work, he was relieved to hear I'd been going to the gym every day. Luke hadn't started competing in strongman at that point, but he already knew plenty about lifting weights. And he saw I had something special. Six months after my first visit, I was doing the whole stack on the lat pulldown, where you sit on a bench, reach up and pull the bar down. I enjoyed that competitive element, the fact there were loads of different machines, for different parts of the body, and I could measure myself against other people.

I loved the feeling of pushing myself and improving. I loved having control over my body, manipulating my shape with different exercises and food. After a year's training, I'd put on a huge amount of bulk. People would stop and stare at me in the street. I even got Mum to take some photos of me, lifting my top up and showing off my new six-pack. I'd show people photos of me before I discovered the gym and they'd think it was a different person.

Growing up, my heroes were Rangers greats Ally McCoist and Paul Gascoigne, and Brazilian legends Pelé, Ronaldinho and Roberto Carlos. They made playing football look so easy. But now I had pictures of five-time World's Strongest Man Mariusz Pudzianowski and American champion Derek Poundstone on my bedroom wall. And I was more intrigued by their physiques than their strength – they weren't barrel-shaped, like a lot of strongmen, they looked like comic-book superheroes. I also loved Arnold Schwarzenegger, because he turned bodybuilding into an art form, and I'd spend hours watching videos about him on YouTube. I was fascinated by anyone who was successful, whatever field they were in. I hoped their positivity would rub off on me.

• • •

When I was 17, a mate asked if I wanted to go to the Belladrum music festival in Beauly. My first thought was, 'How the heck am I supposed to do that, I can't even stay overnight at your house.' But instead of saying no, I decided to set myself a wee goal. I thought, 'I'll get myself as muscly as possible, so I can take my top off if it's hot.' I also went on a strict diet, so by the time of the festival, I was shredded. The fact I'd had my eyes lasered, so I no longer had to wear glasses, made me feel even more confident.

That festival was a pivotal moment in my life. Suddenly, I loved people looking at me. I loved people giving me compliments, telling me I looked like Superman. And it was where I met my first girlfriend and future wife Sinead.

Sinead's friends had their photo taken with me, simply because I was so big. I wasn't bulky like I am now, but I was well over 6ft. Sinead wasn't interested, even when I asked if she wanted a photo of just the two of us. But the following day, she tagged me in some pictures on Facebook. I sent her a message, asked if she wanted to go to the gym with me and gave her my number. And, to my surprise, she said yes.

I thought Sinead would dump me when I told her about my autism, but she said she liked me for who I was. I still put off telling Mum about Sinead, because we were complete opposites – me awkward and shy, her confident and lively – and I was scared of things going wrong. But I couldn't keep it a secret for long. Whenever Mum dropped me off somewhere, she'd ask who I was meeting. At first, I'd tell her I was just meeting friends. But she eventually wore me down, like mums do. When I finally told her I had a girlfriend, her face lit up. She could see I was happy, which made her happy beyond belief.

Mum and Dad loved Sinead from the moment they met her, which put me at ease. Sinead's parents were the same with me. I was painfully shy around them at first, but they soon accepted me into the family. They were two more positive people to add to the growing list.

It was all very well being confident in the gym, but I still wasn't doing much else. However, because Sinead was able to do stuff I found challenging, we dovetailed perfectly. Sinead was so outgoing, and always doing stuff with her friends, so I was quickly absorbed into her world. Sinead was also a very mature young woman, because she'd had to do a lot of things for herself growing up. I wasn't surprised when she became a care worker, because I was like a big baby in the relationship. She didn't always go easy on me, though. Sometimes she'd day, 'You're doing such and such, whether you like it or not. You're not ten years old, Tom, you're a grown man!' I usually did as I was told, because I knew she cared for me and it would be good for both of us.

Things moved so quickly. From believing I'd live with my parents forever, I moved in with Sinead within a year of meeting her. I remember sitting in our house and thinking, 'Wow, never in a million years did I think things would turn out like this.' And I could trace it all back to that first day in the gym with Luke.

People are always saying 'such and such changed my life', and sometimes you wonder if they're exaggerating for effect. But in my case, it's true. If Luke hadn't dragged me down to the gym, I'd still be looking for a purpose in life. And there's no way I'd have been confident enough to go to a music festival and stroll around with my top off. Sinead's friends wouldn't have wanted to have their photo taken with me, Sinead wouldn't have tagged me on Facebook and I'd probably still be single, playing Xbox in my childhood bedroom.

The gym was my substitute school. It gave me confidence and taught me how to interact with people. The gym was the first place I accepted feeling uncomfortable. It gave me a routine. I'd wake up at the same time every day, go to the gym at the same time, eat at the same time, go to bed at the same time. The gym even taught me some maths, which had been a mystery to me. At school, I wasn't interested in learning times tables and stuff like that, because I couldn't see the point. But in the gym, I had to learn, because I needed to know what I was lifting. Not that I realised I was learning all this stuff, because I was having so much fun.

I found sitting in a classroom, staring at textbooks for hours on end, mind-numbingly boring. And it was clear from an early age that I was never going to do anything with geography or history. Plus, I hated being told what to do, even by my mum. That didn't mean I was a bad kid – it just meant I was different.

As Luke has already said, there were lots of other kids in the same boat, who felt uncomfortable in that kind of rigid school environment. They usually came from poor backgrounds or dysfunctional families or had other problems to deal with. Instead of being fed the usual dry academic subjects, it would have made such a difference if they could have been encouraged to do something they enjoyed, something they might have excelled at, something that might have given them a fulfilling, happy life.

Even kids who thrived at school were let down by the system. I know plenty of people who got good grades, went to university and now work in pretty uninspiring jobs. As far as I'm concerned, they were sold a lie and wasted a big chunk of their lives. Getting a degree isn't a prerequisite or a guaranteed path to fulfilling your ambitions.

Sinead made me happy, but I'd worked out that never being happy in the gym was best for me. That might sound strange, but if you're happy in the gym, you're probably not aiming high enough. The hard path is the only path that leads to improvement. And with Luke as my coach, telling me exactly what to do, I progressed far quicker than I thought I would. While most other people were concentrating on upper body stuff, because all they wanted to do was look good in a T-shirt, I was also doing lots of squats and deadlifts. As a result, my whole body was getting stronger, not just my chest, arms and shoulders.

When I was 18 or 19, Luke took me to Peter Macdonald-Brown's gym in Inverness. This was just before he started competing in strongman. And when I saw Luke flipping giant tyres and tossing kegs around, I said to him, 'Why haven't you shown me this before?!' When I started doing all that stuff as well, I thought, 'Wow, this is cool. Lifting logs and cars is a totally different buzz to watching myself lift dumbbells in the mirror.' I felt like a superhero in a movie, doing stuff mere mortals wouldn't even dream of.

In 2013, which was roughly three years on from our first day in the gym together, I travelled down to Dumfries to watch Luke win Scotland's Strongest Man. During an intermission, I won the crowd challenge, which consisted of holding up two beams. I was one of the last to go and beat a couple of lads who'd competed in Highland's Strongest Man. That's when the fire inside me turned into an inferno. After that, I told Sinead I was never going out partying again. As you can imagine, she was over the moon about that.

In 2014, when I was only 19, I entered the qualifiers for Scotland's Strongest Man. I was so, so nervous. Fortunately, the crowds were pretty sparse in those minor events. It was really just a bunch of lads lifting in a gym. And with Luke competing alongside me, and Mum, Dad and Sinead cheering me on, I managed to hold things together and reach the final (despite dropping a log on my face and chipping a tooth).

There were a lot more people at the final, which was even more overwhelming. But just before it started, Sinead said to me, 'Just do what you do in the gym. Enjoy yourself.' In the last event, the Atlas Stones, I had to beat a guy to make sure Luke won the title. I did that and ended up finishing fifth. Afterwards, I thought, 'Geez, I can actually lift weights …'

I followed that up by winning the Under-23 UK's Strongest Man two years running, as well as finishing third in the senior UK's Strongest Man in 2015 (just so you know, UK's Strongest Man is not the same as Britain's Strongest Man). That's when I came to a fork in the road.

I realised I was pretty much the perfect build to be a successful strongman. I was 6ft 8in tall, which is a big advantage in events like the Atlas Stones, where you have to lift things onto high platforms. I weighed about 25 stone, which comes in very handy when pulling trucks or buses. I had a huge wing-span of 6ft 10in, which is great for events like the keg toss. I had very long fingers, all the better for gripping things. I had really long legs, which suited moving events. I was naturally fast – when I was at school, I could do the 100m quicker than anyone else. I had gigantic feet, which were good for balance and stability.

There are disadvantages to being so big, because shorter levers are more suited to pressing and squatting. But I'd just work harder at those events. And the fact is that most of the time in strongman, a man mountain will beat a smaller guy, even if the smaller guy is a superior athlete and technician.

Having taken all that into consideration, I thought, 'If I can do this on the UK stage, why can't I do it on the European stage? Or even the world stage? Why not think as big as possible?' But that was only going to happen if I lived and breathed strongman – and not much else. I had Sinead to think of and bills to pay, so it wasn't going to be easy. But that's just how it had to be.

Or so I thought.

5

PART-TIME STRONGMAN

LUKE

On the face of it, life was great. I had a good job, a long-term girlfriend, my own house, a nice car and a hobby I loved so much it wasn't really a hobby. I'm sure people looked at me and thought, 'That lad has got life sussed.' In truth, I didn't have life sussed at all.

Let's start with that hobby I loved so much it wasn't really a hobby. True, I was officially a strongman – and utterly consumed by it – but I was winging it. For a start, my body wasn't the right shape. I was still quite slim around the waist, more a bodybuilder than a strongman. I struggled to pick stuff up and move it. I needed to eat more, get more thickness and improve my core strength. And I soon learned that all those health and safety guidelines about the 'proper' way to lift stuff didn't apply to strongmen.

When you look at a strongman lifting stones or sandbags, you'll notice his back is curved, not straight. If it's a weirdly shaped object, like an anvil, he'll have to jiggle it to get it in the right position, and most of the weight will end up rested on one arm. A strongman also does a lot of twisting, because that's what the events demand. A health and safety officer would have a fit if he saw me lifting like that on a rig, but it goes to show how adaptable bodies are. To lift the huge weights we lift, we have to do it the wrong way. The paradox being, it's 100 per cent the right way *if* you've trained your body to do it.

I finished seventh in my first UK's Strongest Man in 2013, and well down the field in my first Britain's Strongest Man in Gateshead. But I couldn't really complain, because I hadn't practised most of the events. Gateshead was the first time I'd ever done a yoke, which is a bar across your back with two massive weights on either end. The overall weight was 450kg – and we had to pick it up and run with it.

Now is probably a good time to give you an idea of what all these massive weights are comparable to. Ten kilograms is a mountain bike; 50kg is a bag of cement; 100kg is a giant panda; 200kg is an upright piano; 300kg is a grizzly bear; 400kg is a racehorse; 450kg, which is what the yoke in Gateshead weighed, is a grand piano. Or a lead coffin. Or, apparently, a single whale testicle.

That yoke was the heaviest thing I'd ever lifted, but at least I didn't finish last. I also did okay in the shield carry and loading race (which involves carrying and loading objects onto a platform – anchors, anvils, sandbags, beer kegs, lobster pots, whatever the organisers fancy). The Atlas Stones also went okay, but I scored no points in the deadlift and log press. I'd been bench-pressing 220kg in the gym, no problem. But doing the standing log press, I was like Bambi on ice. I hadn't been working the right muscles and didn't have the core stability.

After getting those kinds of results, some people might have thought, 'I'm not very good at this. Maybe I should give it up.' But that's not how I felt. Yes, I didn't really know what I was doing. While everyone else was wearing proper weightlifting shoes and support sleeves all over their body, I was wearing a pair of Adidas football trainers and had no supports at all. I didn't know how to warm up properly and was constantly side-eyeing the other guys to see what they were doing. But I was buzzing to be there, competing against all these strongmen I'd only ever seen on TV. And the crowd seemed to take to me, which felt nice. I remember thinking, 'Jesus, this could be something.'

The nearest proper strongman gym to us was in Aberdeen. I went there a couple of times, but it was a two-and-a-half-hour drive from home and not that great anyway. Tom had just started doing Strongman too, and we had no choice but to bite the bullet and buy in our own equipment: a log press, a yoke, an axle bar, a couple of giant weights for the farmer's walk, some giant dumbbells, 500kg of plates and a set of Atlas Stones.

We already had one stone, but it wasn't a proper sphere, because part of it had been sheared off. And it wasn't nice and smooth, like the stones you see on TV – it was pitted with gravel. Whenever I tried to lift it, I'd end up with painful scrapes all down my arms.

Strongman equipment doesn't come cheap – and you don't find it second-hand on Gumtree. We got some Atlas Stones sent up by a company in Wales. They were pretty expensive, with the shipping costing almost as much as the stones. Luckily, Mum bought them as a Christmas present, which was a bit more thoughtful than socks. Dad wasn't best pleased, though, because he'd just had the drive retarred. Whenever we dropped a stone, it would leave a massive dent, as if a meteorite had hit.

The giant dumbbells, which go up to 150kg, are imported from America, and they cost even more than Atlas Stones. But I didn't care about the costs, because I was so passionate about getting better. Getting strong had stopped being a hobby. This wasn't for a bit of a giggle, it was something I *needed* to do, simply couldn't live without. Plus, once you've got that equipment, you never have to replace it. It obviously gets battered and worn, but it's unlikely to break. You'd need a couple of hours with a sledgehammer to put a dent in an Atlas Stone.

Nine times out of ten, the events in a strongman competition are roughly the same. You know there'll be a pressing event – log press, axle press, giant dumbbell press or standing press. There'll also be a deadlift, some kind of throwing event – usually tossing kegs or sandbags – and a moving event, usually either a loading race or a giant's medley, involving a yoke and/ or a farmer's walk. They'll probably also have you pulling a truck or a plane, and the final event will always be the stones.

The organisers will sometimes roll different disciplines into one event – for example, combining moving and pressing – to jazz things up a bit. But they can't throw us any major curveballs, because if they have us doing stuff we haven't trained for, we're more likely to injure ourselves.

I'm sure some fans would like to see more variety, but the organisers realise they have to look after their athletes. Besides, I don't see other sports chopping and changing every competition. Imagine if football had different-sized goals every tournament, or used balls of different weights, or kept moving the penalty spot around. People would think it was ridiculous, and rightly so.

Each event requires lots of variations in training. Take the loading race as an example. There are so many different combinations, you never know what they might have you lifting, dragging and carrying. So you've got to make sure every single muscle in your body is properly prepared.

Mum and Dad's house had a garage, which belonged to the gardener when the land was an estate, and we turned that into a wee gym. We'd be in that garage every night, and, after a while, the floor looked just like Dad's drive. We'd attempt a deadlift, and one end of the bar would be lower than the other, because the floor was uneven, thanks to the impact of heavy weights being repeatedly dropped onto it. But we didn't have a choice, so we just had to get on with it. And when we competed on flat surfaces, we felt like footballers who usually play on a turnip field suddenly playing at Wembley.

I also started paying a lot more attention to what I was eating. When I started out in strongman, I was only putting away about 4,000 calories a day and eating very clean. Then I found out that Eddie Hall, the best strongman in Britain, put away more than double that, including a whole cheesecake and a curry some nights.

So, when I was offshore, I'd ask the guy who ran the kitchen to pile my plates up high. I'd look like Henry VIII, tucking into a joint of meat and a hill of potatoes and vegetables, all smothered in gravy. I'd follow that with a big pudding and also take some fruit to my room. Later, I'd sneak down and eat the nightshift dinner, so I was eating four meals a day, sometimes five.

None of it was ideal. If I'd quit my day job and started doing strongman full-time after those first few competitions, I might have got better much quicker. But there's another way of looking at it. Because I did it the hard way, and served an extended apprenticeship, I appreciate my current situation so much more. And maybe if I'd gone full-time earlier, I'd have burned out by now, instead of being a regular player on the biggest stage in my late thirties. Plus, if I hadn't had a job, and one that paid well, I wouldn't have been able to buy all the gear anyway.

• • •

Of course, having a kid brother training alongside me was a huge advantage. And a big relief. Tom's early teenage years were tough. The only time I ever saw him happy was when he played football. I have such fond memories of Tom, me, Harry and Dad playing two against two in the garden, mainly because Tom didn't seem to have a worry in the world. But I wasn't surprised that he never made a career out of it. He'd get nervous on the football field and he lacked aggression. He towered over everyone else but was reluctant to impose himself. People would shout at him, 'Jesus, Tom, push them back!' It must have been frustrating for his coaches and teammates, but he just didn't have it in him.

I dragged Tom him to the gym when he was 16 and he already had the raw ingredients of a strongman. He was skinny, but 6ft 5in, with size 14 feet. Mum was having to get his trainers imported from America. The previous Christmas, she'd bought ten pairs, including five of the same kind, which must have cost a fortune.

That first time at the gym, Tom was very uncomfortable, barely said a word. Looked at one way, it's amazing he stuck at it. Looked at another, it wasn't really a surprise. School wasn't Tom's thing, because he never found anything he loved there, apart from football. In contrast, the gym was the perfect environment for him to thrive in, almost like his greenhouse.

The first time I went offshore, I wondered if Tom would stick at it without me by his side. Thankfully, a good friend of mine took him under his wing while I was away. I heard that when Tom first started coming in without me, he'd say two words the entire time he was there: 'hi' and 'bye'. But after a month or so, Tom started coming out of his shell. By the time I returned to the gym, he was relaxed like I'd never seen him before, which was lovely to see. He was talking to the other lads about motivational gym videos he'd watched on YouTube. He was laughing and joking. His head was held high, his shoulders were back and he exuded purpose. And he was already one of the strongest in the place.

After that, whenever I was offshore, I started getting messages from lads telling me about Tom's latest feat of strength. I remember being told he'd just deadlifted 300 kilos and thinking, 'Bloody hell, my wee brother's going to be an absolute monster ...' And when we started training together in our wee gym in Mum and Dad's garden, Tom really started shifting through the gears. I started to think he might become something very special indeed.

Tom would take the barbell outside and deadlift in the pouring rain, even in the snow. It was like something from a *Rocky* movie – there was something very pure and joyful about it. He was just over the moon to be doing what he loved, whatever the conditions. Never mind his natural size and strength – one year or so into training, that lanky kid had turned into a 6ft 8in, 20-odd-stone beast, with size 17 feet – that love he had for the sport was the key ingredient.

When I started winning competitions, I was very vocal about Tom. I'd grab the mic and say, 'I'm strong, but wait till you see my brother! He's coming, and he's going to be the best in the world!' Then when he finished second behind me at Scotland's Strongest Man in 2015, setting a new national deadlift record of 382kg, I knew he was going to be untouchable. But while I was thrilled by Tom's progress, I was even more wrapped up in myself.

I don't think anyone had won Highland's Strongest Man and Scotland's Strongest Man at their first attempts, and Britain's Strongest Man was shown on TV. I remember watching myself on Britain's Strongest Man for the first time, seeing myself on the same stage as lads like Terry Hollands, a former champion and World's Strongest Man veteran. And I thought, 'Wow, this is really quite surreal.'

In 2014, I finished seventh in Britain's Strongest Man, this time scoring points in the log press and deadlift and winning the loading race. The following year, I finished sixth. I'd been calling myself the strongest man in the North Sea for years. Now I was a yearly fixture on national TV, and Scotland's Strongest Man three times over. That kind of success can go to a man's head.

In my early days in strongman, I didn't think winning was enough, I thought I also needed to carve a niche for myself. I was relatively lean, so whenever I competed, I'd wear the tightest shorts possible and pull off my shirt to show everyone my six-pack. I'd get wolf whistles, so commentators started calling me, 'Luke Stoltman, the ladies' choice.' I was good in front of a microphone, articulate, usually with something funny to say. I didn't think much more would come of my strongman career, certainly didn't think it was a potential business. So, I suppose I thought I might as well have fun with it.

It's not like Mum was going to take me aside and tell me to stop showing off. She absolutely loved it, bless her. She had a load of T-shirts made up, bearing the legend: 'Luke Stoltman – Scotland's Strongest Man'. And that was before I'd won it for the first time! The guy who printed them, from Inverness market, probably bought a house with the amount of money Mum spent on T-shirts. And they got brighter and brighter with every competition, ending up being fluorescent pink. Let's just say Mum was confident in my ability.

I was a naturally shy boy from a small place in the middle of nowhere, where people just went about their business with no fuss. So, to be something of a face around town was brilliant. And without getting too Freudian, I'd probably been starved of attention since I was a kid. I wouldn't say I suffered – that would be too dramatic. But Dad was away a lot, and most of Mum's attention was focused on Tom. Now, I could walk into a bar, see a good-looking woman and feel confident approaching her. Especially if I had a few beers inside me.

Sometimes, I'd do a competition on the Saturday, get home on the Sunday and head back offshore on the Monday. Out on the rigs, reality would crash into me, like a great wave. I wouldn't say I was depressed, but I did end up hating that job. I could be stuck on a rig for weeks on end. Some of my colleagues were great, but some of them were miserable as anything, constantly moaning. Surveying is a skilled job, and an important one, but it's not exactly thrilling. You'll certainly never hear a wee kid say, 'I'd like to work offshore when I grow up, because I'd like to be away from home for a month, sharing a bunk bed with a big, sweaty, horrible bloke.'

But most of all, I didn't like working on the rigs because every day was the same and it was stopping me doing what I loved. The thought I'd probably be doing it until I was well into my sixties made me feel a bit sick. My only comfort was the gym. At least when I was in the gym, I was working on becoming a better person. Yes, I was stuck on a rig in the middle of the sea. But I felt like I was progressing. Just don't mention the time I walked into a gym and saw a colleague running on the treadmill in his Y-fronts. I remember thinking, 'Just don't make eye contact and you'll probably be fine ...'

Sometimes, I'd dream I was back home, training in a proper gym, nice and content. Then I'd wake up and realise I was out in the North Sea, with another mind-numbing shift ahead of me. I'd think about the rain coming in sideways, the wind almost taking my head off, the smell of grease, all that heavy clanking. And I'd want to pull the duvet back over my head.

I think I was looking to fill a bit of a void. I knew if I went to the pub, I'd be in the limelight again. I was Scotland's Strongest Man, and earning decent money offshore too. The success also gave me a bit of a sense of entitlement.

Remember that long-term relationship I mentioned, the one that seemed so solid? That went down the pan. Looking back, most people probably thought I was a decent enough guy. But I was very self-absorbed and wasn't too worried about who I hurt. All in all, I wasn't a nice person.

I can make excuses. I was still a young man, lacking in confidence, not really knowing who I was. And I'd have been mad not to enjoy my newfound fame and success. Lots of people wanted to know me. Being young and naive, I didn't realise a lot of them were fake, that they just wanted something from our relationship. But it still makes me cringe, thinking about some of the things I did.

It was only when Tom started competing in strongman that I got back on the right path. Before then, it had been all about me, but now I had a project of sorts – making Tom, a brother I loved, into the best person he could possibly be.

6

THE BIGGEST LOSS

TOM

While Luke was dipping his toe into the strongman world, I was still trying to find meaning in life, other than my beloved Rangers. I'd had a fair few jobs since leaving school. I did labouring and landscaping with my brother-in-law. I put up fences with my uncle, which was brutal. I did a bit of security work on the door at pubs and clubs. I worked in a supermarket, stacking shelves. Then I fell into a job doing security work on a building site. I was one of those blokes who sits in a wee cabin, all on their own for 12 hours a day. It wasn't tough physically, but it was mind-numbing.

Meanwhile, Mum wasn't doing too well. She was suffering from severe chest pains, but when she told her GP about them, he didn't bother doing any scans. He said it was probably something called Bornholm disease, which is a viral infection that causes stabbing pains and usually disappears without the need for treatment.

But ten months passed, and the pains hadn't gone away. In fact, they had got worse. That got everyone worried. Mum was a very hardy woman. She'd brought up five kids, often without Dad, so she never really had the time to get sick. She spent hours doing back-breaking work in the garden and was as strong as most men. So, when Mum said she was in pain, you knew it must be bad.

Even when Mum told her GP she was in agony, he still refused to send her for a scan. Instead, he gave her more pain-killers. She'd already had so many of those she almost rattled when she walked. Eventually, the GP agreed to send her for an X-ray. Nothing showed up and she was given the all-clear, but the pains didn't go away. In the end, Dad and Luke decided to send her private.

Mum's CT scan revealed she had terminal cancer, which had started in her breast before spreading to her liver and spine. The doctors said she might only have six months to live. I was kept in the dark for a while, because she knew I'd take it particularly badly. But I kept asking questions, because there was obviously something very wrong with her, and eventually she told me.

I'd always been Mum's main focus, because of my autism. She'd never given up on me having a normal life, when plenty of other mums would have. And now she was close to dying. I was lucky to have the support of Sinead and her family, but the thought of losing Mum was almost unbearable. And I kept thinking, 'Why is this happening to her, the nicest person in the world?'

Thankfully, things were at least going well on other fronts. Sinead and I tied the knot in 2015, three years after meeting at the music festival. A few days before the wedding, we were ambushed. Don't worry, nothing bad happened. Up in the Highlands, there is a tradition called 'blackening', which is when family and friends throw eggs, flour and sauces at the bride and groom before parading them through the local community.

Poor Mum might have been very ill, but I don't think I've ever seen her so happy. A truck took us from Invergordon to Alness, Sinead's hometown, and loads of people came out to wish us luck. We looked like freaks and probably stank to high heaven – eggs with tomato ketchup smells nice on your plate, not so much when it's dripping off your face. Then again, we apparently got off lightly: if we'd got married in medieval times, we might have been tarred and feathered.

The wedding day was just as memorable, like something from a dream. Sinead looked beautiful, stacks of people came and the celebrations went on until the wee hours. Being honest, it's not something I'd have even dared to dream of before I met Sinead. From thinking I'd amount to nothing to marrying an incredible woman in the space of a few years, it was just so surreal.

I was also getting stronger and stronger, which Luke had a lot to do with. You always want to beat your brother, whether it's playing Monopoly or lifting weights. At the very least, you don't want to be embarrassed by him. And people would always comment on how competitive we were in the gym.

Luke would always want to do one more rep than me, and vice versa. But the competition was never unfriendly. Luke would stand over me shouting, 'One more rep! And another!' He wanted to beat me, but he also wanted me to get better, so that I could push him to greater heights. We were competitive, but we were also working together.

He'd certainly never tell me to stop lifting if he thought I was overdoing things, because he knew it was pointless. I'd say to Luke, 'I'll only stop lifting if a doctor tells me to, or if I collapse and die.' That's how I thought a strongman had to think.

I also trained with two other man mountains who competed in Scotland's Strongest Man, so when I started competing at junior level in 2016, I had a big physical edge over my rivals. That's why people kept saying I was the future of the sport, and why I thought I was going to win every junior title there was. Unfortunately, I was still far too frail mentally. If I didn't do well in an event, I'd flip out and the rest of the competition would be a write-off. If I finished last in an event, I'd quit.

When I first competed in the Under-23 World Championship, I was leading throughout. But I made a hash of the final event and finished fifth. It was difficult to get my head around. I probably thought I was better than I was and didn't show enough respect. I also found the pressure very difficult to deal with. When I was done with the juniors, I thought, 'Jesus, I haven't exactly taken the world by storm. Maybe I'm not cut out for this sport after all?'

In 2016, I finished second behind Luke in Scotland's Strongest Man for the second year running – and this time it was even closer. But by the end of the year, I thought I'd never lift another thing. Mum, fighter that she was, had stuck around a lot longer than six months, but she was in terrible pain and in and out of hospital. Her deterioration was awful to witness. She'd been such a tough, strong woman, and now she struggled to do anything for herself. I felt sad and depressed and demotivated. I even refused to fly out for a competition. Mum tried to persuade me to go, but I didn't want to leave her.

Then, on 13 November 2016, Mum passed away. The last thing she said to me was, 'Achieve whatever you want to.' That just about summed Mum up, spending her final moments on earth worrying about me. But it would be a while before I felt up to doing anything, let alone following my dream.

I found it incredibly difficult to accept she had been taken away so early. She didn't drink or smoke or do drugs. She kept herself fit. She was a wonderful, kind lady. It didn't seem fair, and it didn't seem real.

I didn't grieve openly, didn't even discuss my feelings with Sinead. But I was only sleeping a couple of hours a night. And when I started taking sleeping pills, I'd have horrendous nightmares. Instead of talking, I drank to forget. I'd go out partying a few days during the week, and at the weekend I'd have a 24-hour session without any sleep. Then I'd vegetate all day Sunday, before doing it all again. I was still managing to train, just about. But the gym was a distant second to the pub in my list of priorities. As for competing, I didn't give a stuff.

Mum was always very supportive when it came to strongman, but she thought there were more important things in life. I'd say to her, 'I want to be a successful strongman and do you proud.' And she'd reply, 'That's great, Tom. But it's more important to me that you're independent, have a good wife and your own home.' So, I was relieved I'd done all that before Mum passed. But I also thought, 'Now Mum's gone, what's the point in carrying on in strongman?' I was mostly doing strongman for Mum – and now she'd never see me win anything.

Mum's death must have hit Dad hard, but I didn't really see him grieve either. He's a tough Highlander, and men of his generation tend not to let their emotions hang out. So, while he must have had lots of bad days, he grieved in private. And he was a tower of strength in public because he didn't want to make us kids any sadder. As a family, we made the garden into a memorial for Mum, while Dad ploughed a lot of his energy into doing up the house. He even stopped smoking, because he knew that would have made Mum proud.

For months, I almost didn't believe that Mum was gone. I took a sunflower with me wherever I went, because they were her favourite. I found that comforting. But it was only after I got a tattoo of Mum on my arm, on the stairway to heaven and holding a sunflower, that I started getting my life back on track. It's difficult to put into words, but it now felt that Mum was with me at all times. And because she was always with me, I had to go out and achieve my goals, like she'd told me to do on her deathbed. Otherwise, I'd be betraying her.

From that point on, I tried not to think of Mum when she was ill, but the vibrant woman she was before that. But I talked about her a lot, because it made it seem like she was still around. And every time I lifted something, it felt like Mum was pushing with me, with every ounce of her strength.

• • •

I cut down on my drinking and partying, stopped having night-mares and refocused on the gym. But before that, a few weeks after Mum's passing, I competed down in Newcastle, finish-ing fourth in the Ultimate Strongman World Championships. And the following month, I made my debut in Britain's Strongest Man.

Luke was by my side, trying to make me feel comfortable as always. And I knew I could outlift most of my fellow compet-itors in my gym. Unfortunately, we weren't in my gym, and I found the situation completely overwhelming.

Before graduating to UK level, I thought strongman was a backyard sport hardly anyone watched. But there was a big audi-ence in Doncaster, plus cameras and lighting everywhere. I spent the whole week leading up to the competition worrying about being interviewed. When the time came, I clammed up and Luke had to talk for me. Straight afterwards, I had to lie down.

By the morning of the competition, I was mentally drained. I kept looking at the queues outside, all these people who'd come to see me. Waiting to be introduced to the crowd, I was shaking backstage, thinking, 'I can't go out there ...' And when I did go out there, being in the spotlight terrified me.

I still managed to finished sixth out of a field of 12, which wasn't bad for my debut. Luke finished two places ahead of me, and there were some very good lads below me, including Adam Bishop, who'd competed in World's Strongest Man the previous couple of years. But it had been an ordeal.

That was the year Eddie Hall won his fourth title on the trot, and seeing a guy who was only 6ft 2in – Eddie claims to be an inch taller than that, but no-one believes him – smashing the field like he did was inspirational. Eddie won three of the six events and came second in the other three. Mind you, Luke beat him in the stones, and was only a couple of points off the podium.

Our performances in Doncaster meant we both qualified for World's Strongest Man in Botswana in 2017, which was an even bigger eye-opener. A few years earlier, I was a lanky teenager shifting weights in a council gym in Invergordon. Now, I was sharing the biggest stage with strongman legends like four-time champions Brian Shaw and Žydrūnas 'Big Z' Savickas, as well as Iceland's Hafthór 'Thor' Björnsson, who'd been runner-up twice. And Gaborone, where the competition took place, was absolutely buzzing.

Thank God Luke was there with me, because I was a big bag of nerves. I was looking at all these beasts, thinking, 'What the heck am I doing here? I'm just a kid. Maybe I should go back to the wee cabin on the building site.'

I was actually in the same heat as Brian – and he pumped me! While I dragged a 350kg cart loaded with two 100kg sacks just shy of four metres, Brian dragged it almost nine. While I managed three reps of the 158kg log lift, Brian managed five. While Brian lifted five Fingal's fingers – massive steel poles weighing up to 170kg – I lifted three and tore my rotator cuff. I withdrew before the final two events, meaning I finished fifth out of six and didn't qualify for the finals.

But what an experience for a 22-year-old. Watching the likes of Brian, Big Z and Thor was all the inspiration I needed to keep improving. World's Strongest Man was a whole different ball game from British level, like the Premier League compared to League One. I spent a lot of time observing how the big guns went about their work. I learned what it was like to compete in a week-long event, rather than just for a day. And after the nerves had died down a bit, I was able to enjoy it. I came away from Gaborone thinking, 'If I keep training hard, and get the right guidance, I'll be a Premier League fixture for years to come.'

Amazingly, Eddie managed to beat the lot of them in the finals, which upset a few people. Afterwards, there were loads of conspiracies doing the rounds. People were saying Eddie knew the events months in advance, that they were tailored specifically for him, that Thor was cheated out of a point on the Viking press. There was even a rumour that someone applied the brakes during Brian's plane pull. All of it was nonsense. Eddie put the work in and deserved his win. Not that anyone knew about it for months, because we all had to sign non-disclosure contracts, so most people didn't know who'd won before it was shown on TV at Christmas.

A few months later, I finished second behind Laurence Shahlaei at UK's Strongest Man. Laurence had been around the block a few times and won Britain's and Europe's Strongest Man, so that was another decent result.

I was also starting to feel a bit more comfortable in a competition environment, although not entirely. Because strongmen are all doing the same unusual thing, it's like a very exclusive club, or even a family. Everyone respects each other, because they know how hard everyone else is grafting in the gym. Everyone wants to win, but there's no hostility. When I appeared on the scene, my rivals' attitude was, 'Wow! This is gonna be exciting to watch.' Rather than, 'Jesus, look at the size of this bloke, he's gonna end up killing us.'

From the beginning, I had rivals cheering me on and giving me tips. If I recorded a personal best, they'd slap me on the back and congratulate me. After a competition, we'd all go out for a meal and a drink. And it didn't matter who'd finished first or last, everyone was treated the same. There were no alpha males trying to lord it over everyone else. It was a load of big lads in the same small boat, all rowing in the same direction.

I seemed to be on an unstoppable rise. Famous strongmen were calling me the next big thing, including Eddie Hall. I even had a nickname – 'The Albatross'. But the pressure that comes with great expectation was about to bring me crashing to the ground. Just like the old days on the football pitch.

In 2018, I was one of the favourites for Britain's Strongest Man, and I desperately wanted to win it. Some readers might think Britain's Strongest Man is a minor event, not that important in the grand scheme of things. But it's been won by some of the greatest strongmen ever – Geoff Capes, two-time World's Strongest Man; Jamie Reeves, world champion in 1989; Wales's Gary Taylor, world champion in 1994; Terry Hollands, who'd had two podium finishes at World's Strongest Man; and, of course, Eddie Hall. World's Strongest Man is obviously the most prestigious competition, but Britain's Strongest Man isn't too far behind.

But having lived and breathed the sport for the last few years, I got pumped by everyone and finished last. That competition in Sheffield was a disaster from start to finish. I managed only two lifts in the log ladder (Eddie Hall managed 13), one rep in the deadlift (Eddie managed 15) and eight seconds in the front hold (Eddie managed 58!). After the front hold, I ripped my belt off, threw it away and stormed off. Backstage, Sinead tried to persuade me to do the final event, the stones. But I wasn't interested. I never wanted to compete in strongman again.

I felt like a fake, because I was unable to do what I did in the gym in a competition. Negative thoughts were getting stuck in my head when they should have been flying over it. I thought I was embarrassing myself, Sinead and my family. I thought that unless I won, I was letting everyone down. I couldn't work out why I'd failed so spectacularly when people like Eddie Hall had been talking me up. Surely if Eddie thought I was good, it must be true? After all, he wasn't just some random punter – he was the World's Strongest Man!

I think all that praise had probably made me a bit arrogant, or at least complacent. I thought, 'If Eddie thinks I'm great, I don't have to worry.' Looking back, the idea that I was going to turn up and beat all these seasoned professionals was madness. I was constantly battling nerves as well as my rivals, which left me utterly drained after a couple of events. And I was competing with a dodgy shoulder, following the injury in Botswana.

But at the time, it was all very confusing and disheartening. I'd given it everything I had. I'd thought about strongman every hour of every day, stayed at home when my friends were going out and having fun and made Sinead's life a misery at times. And I'd still blown up when it counted.

7

THE
CIRCLE
OF LIFE

LUKE

was working in Newcastle when they did Mum's CT scan, and I knew it was going to reveal something bad. I was driving to the gym when Mum phoned me. Just the way she said hello told me it was going to be terrible news. That was the worst conversation I've ever had. By a million miles. To hear my normally sunny, optimistic Mum so upset – and to know she wouldn't be around for much longer – was utterly devastating.

When a loved one tells you something like that, you instinctively think you need to spring into action. But I was stuck down in Newcastle, 300 miles from Invergordon, and felt utterly useless. The job still had another three weeks to run, and Mum told me not to come home until I'd finished. That was typical of her. But I really didn't understand how I was supposed to react.

I'm sure some people would have gone home anyway. Others would have turned their car around, gone back to their hotel and cried on their bed. But I went on and trained as if nothing had happened. I felt awful after I'd finished my session. But I suppose that was just a coping mechanism.

I worked as usual for the next few days and was out for dinner with a mate when I received a call from my sister. Mum had collapsed, there was blood in her urine and she'd been rushed to hospital. So I jumped in my car, pointed it towards Invergordon and stepped on it, expecting the worst.

Mum had bumped her kidney, which explained the blood in her urine. Thank God she wasn't about to die. But I'd never seen her in such a state. She was broken down, beside herself. I was her eldest so had always felt particularly protective of her. And to see her like that was almost unbearable.

But after I left the hospital, sadness turned to anger. Doctors do wonderful things, which is why they're held in such high regard. But maybe if Mum's GP had spotted the cancer in its early stages, she would have had a fighting chance.

I drove to the GP's surgery, marched up to reception and said, 'I want to speak to Dr So and So.' The receptionist asked me what it was about, and I replied, 'He's misdiagnosed my mum for almost a year and now she's got terminal cancer. I'd like to have a conversation with him about it.'

This receptionist looked quite scared. While she was on the phone to the GP's office, she probably had her finger on the alarm button under her desk. But after a tense few seconds, she put the phone down and told me the doctor must be out. Maybe she was lying. Maybe he'd seen me coming and run away. Whatever went on, it was probably for the best.

Once I'd calmed down a bit, I decided to speak to a lawyer; I'd see if I could get Mum some justice in court. But when I met up with this medical malpractice lawyer in Edinburgh, he told me there was nothing he could do. Apparently, he had people coming to him all the time with similar stories, and it would probably be impossible to prove that Mum had had cancer for months before the diagnosis, rather than days or weeks. I understood what he was saying, but it wasn't easy to swallow.

When it looked like Mum didn't have long left, I decided to take some time off work. I ended up spending six weeks with her, and I'm so glad I did.

It wasn't easy seeing her get sicker and sicker. Having spinal cancer could have left her paralysed, so she had to get regular injections to prevent that from happening. Mum called those injections 'a little bit sore', which was no doubt a euphemism for 'absolutely agonising'. I vividly recall one time when she was lying on the couch, screaming in pain, because she had a hole in the lining of her bowel. When the ambulance came and whisked her to hospital, I thought that might have been it. But the following morning, she was back on her feet and insisting everything was fine. That's what an incredibly strong woman she was.

Watching Mum go through that put a lot of stuff into perspective. It made me realise that doing strongman is manufactured pain, pain you recover from quickly. What Mum was experiencing was real pain, constant and almost unbearable. I found myself thinking, 'Lifting heavy stuff is nothing compared to what Mum's going through. Jesus, if I can't get through a training session without moaning, I can't be right in the head.'

Dad and I spent hours in the garden, making it as nice as possible. And when I wasn't chopping down trees and planting flowers, I chatted to Mum. They were some of the best times of my life and provided some closure after she passed. Not everyone is that fortunate. Their mum or dad gets ill while they're busy with work or spending time with their own family, which means they never manage to say a proper goodbye and have the conversations they wanted to.

Mum drew up a bucket list – not skydiving or climbing mountains, but more homely stuff like cooking. One day, she decided to make pear tarts for us all. Unfortunately, the morphine was making her slightly delirious. When I went round in the morning, as I did every day, she'd emptied all the eggs into a bowl but put the shells into the mixer, along with the flour and butter. I sat her down, made her a cup of tea, picked the shells out and became overwhelmed with sadness and anger.

The whole situation was just completely unacceptable to me. Us human beings are more technologically advanced than we've ever been, so much effort is ploughed into cancer research yet we can't seem to put much of a dent in that terrible disease. They called Covid a pandemic, but we go through a pandemic every year with cancer, and God knows how many other diseases. It's not right, all these people dying every day. It makes me very frustrated, because there must be a cure out there.

Three or four days after Mum made those pear tarts, she passed away. We were all heartbroken, but it must have been particularly devastating for Tom, because he and Mum were incredibly close. She wasn't just his mum, she was his best friend, his therapist, his closest counsel. She knew Tom better than anyone else in the world, but now she was gone.

Some days Tom would seem fine, others not so much. Sometimes it was impossible to tell. Being in the gym and competing was what he did to feel good about himself. But because he was in so much emotional pain, the idea of doing a four-hour gym session was too much for him. Plus, you need focus as an athlete, and Tom's concentration was shot. So instead of eating the right things and training properly, he thought, 'To hell with it, I'll have a few beers instead.'

I was surprised Tom competed in Newcastle, a few weeks after Mum's passing, because whatever he'd done, he'd done it for her. And it must have been disconcerting not being able to hear Mum screaming support from the sidelines. But I think Mum's passing eventually made Tom stronger, certainly mentally. He still did strongman to make other people proud. But, deep down, he started doing it for himself. That makes all the difference.

As for me, after a little celebration of her life, I started working again, because Mum wouldn't have wanted me moping about feeling sorry for myself. But I wasn't exactly great at dealing with the grief. Mum had been the centre of everything in our family.

When I was back onshore, I spent a lot of time angry and depressed. I was in a dark hole and couldn't see a way out. Some days, I couldn't get out of bed, let alone leave the house. If someone asked me how I felt, I'd either tell them I was alright or that I didn't want to talk about it. Whenever there was a family event, I'd volunteer to work, because the idea of a family event without Mum seemed so bleak.

I spent a lot of time in therapy, trying to unravel what was going on in my head, and I slowly opened up to other people. I'd been scared of talking, of being heard. I thought it would make me less of a man. But everyone was so supportive, and it made me realise that so many people had been in the same boat and knew what it was to suffer. Then one day, someone said to me, 'Just because your mum isn't here in a physical form, that doesn't necessarily mean you have to stop having a relationship with her.' That made me feel a lot better.

Suddenly, I could feel Mum's presence every day. When I visited Dad, I'd see Mum on her hands and knees in the garden. I'd see her driving past in her old van, beeping her horn, smiling and waving. I'd savour the memories of being with her, instead of trying to block them out. And everything I did, I did with the aim of making Mum proud. And whenever I had to make a decision, I'd ask myself, 'What would Mum think?' To be frank, it stopped me from being an idiot.

In the gym, I was more determined than ever to ignore so-called pain and push through whatever limits I thought I had. When I suffered an injury, I'd think, 'It's nothing really.' Like the time I dropped something on my foot in a competition. I didn't want the medical team to insist on an X-ray and pull me out, so I pretended I was okay, even though my foot was fractured.

I'm very grateful I got to spend so much time with Mum before she went, even though we had some difficult conversations. She'd looked after Tom for so long, and she needed to know I'd carry on her life's work. That was so important to her. But most of all, Mum wanted me to be happy, even though it took me a while to work out what it really meant to be happy.

For ages, I thought being happy meant working like crazy and earning plenty of money. But it doesn't really work like that. Now, I know that happiness is doing something you love for a living. And being happy doesn't mean you're always laughing and joking and dancing a jig. I still get jaded, because life can be monotonous. I still get sad, because bad things happen. That's just the way things have to be, for everyone. But I know there are good times ahead, because I'll make them so. Mum passing away taught me that life is so fragile. You don't know what's going to happen tomorrow, so treat every day as if it's your last. You'll enjoy life a lot more that way.

There's a mental health crisis in Scotland. More consideration should be given to education than treatment. Like telling men it's okay to talk about their problems, that it doesn't make them weak. In fact, it makes you stronger and more of a complete, functioning man. And that focusing on simple things can help you feel better. Like getting out and about in the wilds of Scotland, which are so beautiful and peaceful, my idea of heaven.

There are a lot of isolated communities in the Highlands – even the towns are small. When you're a kid growing up in a place like that, your options can sometimes feel limited. I've thought it would be great to start a charity, offering paths to success that don't require good grades at school or a university education. We would also work a lot on mindset and promoting a healthy mental approach.

Hopefully we could reach some of Scotland's youngsters who are struggling with modern life and all its complications. Tom and I have shown there are lots of different ways to be happy. And I hope we've shown that pretty much anything is attainable, however outlandish it might seem. And we'd certainly tap into our granddad's story, because it's more inspirational than almost anyone's. When kids hear about what he went through, maybe it will make their own lives seem a little less desperate.

• • •

A few years before Mum passed away, I was in the gym when a mate said to me, 'Have you seen this wee bit of stuff that's been training?' At the time, I hadn't. But when I saw her for the first time, I thought, 'Yeah, I get what he means, she *is* pretty tidy …'

Her name was Kushi. She'd only recently moved to the Highlands from London, and was at college with Tom. So, I went up to her and said, 'I hear you know Tom Stoltman. I'm his brother Luke, Scotland's strongest man.' I actually said that, as she often likes to remind me. What an idiot.

I was seeing someone else at the time, as was Kushi, but we both ended up splitting up with our partners. And a couple of years after first meeting in the gym, we went on a date. There soon followed a second date, then a third, and soon we were besotted with each other.

When Kushi went travelling in Australia in 2016, I stayed behind to compete in Scotland's Strongest Man before following her out there. I sold my car to pay for it. After about six weeks, I asked her to marry me before we both headed to Bali. Mum was shocked when I told her. She'd only just got over me splitting with my previous girlfriend.

In April 2015, I had my first experience of World's Strongest Man in Malaysia. I only went as a reserve, but still got a lot out of it. Because I wasn't competing, I spent every evening in the hotel bar. The booze was free, so we'd be there until six or seven in the morning. Thank God none of the competitors pulled out, because I probably would have puked all over the Atlas Stones.

As it was, I got to know a lot of important people in that bar. By then, I'd worked my way up to supervisor offshore and was pretty good at speaking to people. So, in Malaysia, I introduced myself to anyone and everyone: the organisers, the guys who set up all the events, important TV people. Had I not, it would have been easy for them to forget about me. But by making an effort, I was increasing my chances of being invited the following year.

I knew all the British lads, but still didn't have the confidence to chat to the international guys who were competing. I'd been keeping tabs on them for years, since I'd started shifting weights in the gym. My first heroes were bodybuilders like Ronnie Coleman and Jay Cutler. Then I started getting interested in strongmen like Derek Poundstone and the legendary Pole Mariusz Pudzianowski. In Malaysia, I was suddenly standing yards away from two-time champion Brian Shaw from America, reigning champion Žydrūnas 'Big Z' Savickas and Europe's Strongest Man, Thor Björnsson.

Big Z, from Lithuania, is often touted as the greatest strongman of all time. And for good reason. He first competed in World's Strongest Man in 2002, winning it four times and finishing second five times. In his prime he was unbeatable, and he still holds a ridiculous number of world records. Big Z was

40 in Malaysia, very old to be competing in Strongman. But he still had this incredible air of strength and finished just behind Brian, with Thor making up the podium places. To see them in action up close, and take in their size and strength, was incredibly inspirational.

As well as picking up technical tips, I watched how they warmed up and warmed down. I saw how much downtime they had – maybe they'd do one event at eight in the morning and another at three in the afternoon. I noted how they interacted with each other – or didn't. I noted how they psyched themselves up and celebrated. The weather in Malaysia was disgusting – about 40°C and 100 per cent humidity – and I noted how that affected their performance. Despite lifting nothing – apart from a pint glass – I left Malaysia a lot wiser than I had been.

A few months later, I got to compete against Thor for the first time. As often happens in strongman, someone got injured and I was handed a spot in Europe's Strongest Man. Luckily, it was in Leeds, so I could just jump in the car and head down there sharpish. It was the last time a Giants Live event (Giants Live being an official strongman tour) was held outdoors, at Headingley Stadium. And I remember getting a bus from the hotel, with all the other competitors, and seeing big queues outside. We were all buzzing, and that's when I started to feel I was part of something special, and that I belonged in the inner circle.

Thor was – and is – a monster of a man, standing 6ft 9in. That's why they cast him in *Game of Thrones*. We ended up sharing a sponsor and would occasionally go out for dinner together. One time, after a fitness expo in Birmingham, Thor sat down in a restaurant and made his chair disappear. I'd never seen anything like it, it was like a magic trick. I just looked at him and said, 'Jesus, you really are huge!' before falling about laughing.

Thor blitzed the field in Leeds, winning three of the six events (although Eddie Hall was also flying before he had to pull out injured). Not only was Thor huge, and brutally strong, he was also nimble and athletic, as you'd expect of a former basketball player. That meant he was very handy in events that require movement and speed, like the loading race. As for me, I finished joint seventh that day, equal with Terry Hollands, which I was pretty chuffed about.

In August 2015, I had to go to South Korea with work, and this time Kushi followed me out there. We ended up living there for eight months, and spent a bit of time travelling around Asia. When we returned to Scotland, my new house was still being built, so we stayed with Kushi's parents for a little while before moving in together. That was interesting, because the romance had been such a whirlwind that we didn't actually know each other that well. But that soon changed and we set a wedding date for the following June.

We probably wouldn't have got married so soon, but Mum wasn't looking too good. Being the woman she was, she put on a brave face, but she was pretty wrecked. Like Tom and Sinead, Kushi and I were 'blackened' – covered in eggs, flour and God knows what else before being driven around Invergordon in a decorated truck. Mum got a good laugh out of that. And at the wedding, she was running around and snapping away, getting in the way of the official photographer. She even gave interviews to the media. It was so special to have her there, being the same old Mum, despite everything she was going through. And she was thrilled I'd found someone who made me happy.

I'm sure Kushi sometimes wondered how on earth she'd ended up with a strongman. It's a mad situation to find yourself in, that's for sure. Strongman partners travel all over the world, watching their blokes lift heavy stuff, and only they know the emotions involved and the support required. That's probably why strongmen are so close with their partners. In fact, the whole lot of us are like one big travelling family – and quite a strange, dysfunctional one!

I sometimes felt bad, because I had to be pretty selfish as a strongman. Add my day job into the mix and a lot of our relationship was centred on my pursuits. Kushi was always incredibly supportive; she'd been fully on board from the outset and had enjoyed the ride so far. Ultimately, it was about the two of us working well together. It was my responsibility to be as strong as I could in order to provide for us. And Kushi understood why I spent so much time doing what I did, whether it was in the gym or out on the rigs.

She always knew the right things to say – or not to say – when I'd had a bad workout or competition. She knew that when I was emotional or down in the dumps, it was nothing personal. She knew that when she went down to London to see family or friends, I usually wouldn't be able to go with her. She knew that in the few days before a competition, I wouldn't have time for anyone else. Kushi has always been an incredible support.

I know it sounds a bit 'me, me, me'. But sometimes that's how an athlete's relationship has to be, whatever sport they are competing in. On a more positive note, it was lovely having someone who was as thrilled by my successes as I was. It was lovely that I could tell Kushi I'd had a great gym session and she'd be as excited as me (although there was probably some relief mixed in, because it meant I wouldn't be a grumpy bastard when I got home!). Everything about Kushi fitted me perfectly. And everything I did, I did it for both of us. I'd lost one great woman but found another.

8

THE THREE-YEAR PLAN

TOM

After crashing and burning at Britain's Strongest Man in 2018, I took two months off, trying not to think about the sport at all. And it was nice to have a normal life again.

I didn't miss the stress of competing. I liked being able to eat what I wanted. I liked going out whenever I wanted. And eventually I thought, 'Maybe living and breathing strongman was the problem? Maybe living and breathing any one thing isn't good for you, however much you love it?'

When you're autistic, you can become obsessed with routine and specific interests. So, it wasn't easy for me to make the necessary adjustments. But with the help of Sinead and Luke, I worked out that finding a balance was the only option. Either I changed my approach or I'd have to quit. And I really didn't want to quit being a strongman, because it was the one thing I was good at.

I started going to the gym again. But once I was done training, I switched off. I spent time with Sinead, went out with friends, enjoyed life. I managed to find a balance between being 100 per cent committed in the gym and switched-off when I was anywhere else. Everyone needs that balance, whatever they do for a job. Whether you're a strongman, a policeman, a teacher or a lawyer, you need to take time out for yourself, otherwise you'll soon burn out.

That disastrous experience in Sheffield was a blessing in disguise. It made me realise I wasn't as good as I thought. It didn't matter what Eddie Hall or anyone else said about me, I still had a lot of work to do if I wanted to mix it with the best. Laurence Shahlaei, twice Britain's Strongest Man, always says my implosion in Sheffield was the best thing that ever happened to me. He's right. Failures feel terrible when they happen, but they're the key to getting better.

• • •

For my first few years in strongman, Luke had been my unofficial trainer. He designed my programmes, gave me technical advice and told me what to eat. But the higher Luke rose through the ranks, the more he needed to concentrate on himself. Luckily, when I started competing at junior level, I met a guy called Dan Hipkiss. Dan was coaching one of my rivals at the time, but at one competition he said to me, 'If you move your stance in a wee bit, you'll get a better deadlift.' A lot of coaches aren't that generous. Even better, Dan's advice worked. So, I asked if he'd be my coach, and he said yes.

Having finished second behind Luke in Scotland's Strongest Man for three years in a row, I was beginning to wonder if I'd ever beat him. On top of that, people kept asking if I actually wanted to beat him. I think people assumed there was something psychological going on, that I kept losing out of respect for my older brother. Maybe there was something unconscious going on, but suggesting I was deliberately underperforming is very unfair to Luke.

I gave every competition my all, but Luke just had a lot more experience than me. He knew what he had to do to win and was far more consistent. And if I had a bad event, my head would go down and Luke would capitalise on that.

Before Scotland's Strongest Man in 2018, people were suddenly saying, 'Tom Stoltman's obviously not as good as we thought he was. He hasn't got it between the ears.' But I was a different beast by then. I now had a brilliant coach by my side, constantly tweaking things and telling me I could be the best. I also installed a few cameras in the gym and started playing crowd noise through a speaker. I'd get people to move around and speak to me while I was lifting. It was all about trying to replicate a competition environment in training.

All that attention to detail worked, because I blew everyone out of the water, beating Luke into second place by quite a few points. Not only had I won my first senior title, but I'd also toppled my hero. I remember thinking, 'Wow, I've beaten my big brother.' But much better than that, I'd kept the trophy in the family. I only wished Mum could have seen me win it. Had she been there, her screaming would have shattered every window and made half the audience deaf.

There followed a couple of average results in Manchester and Dubai. So just before Christmas 2018, I quit my job as a security guard. I was sitting in the wee cabin thinking, 'I'm only able to give strongman 60 per cent. What if I could give it 100 per cent?' One day I decided the job simply wasn't for me anymore and I handed in my notice, mid-shift.

When I got home, Sinead said to me, 'Why aren't you at work?' And I replied, 'I've quit.' She went mental – and didn't stop going mental for the next two or three days. I did my best to explain why I'd done it. I told her I wanted to do something I loved. I told her I didn't make it in football because I was scared, and I didn't want that to happen again. I told her I could always go back to security, but I only had one shot at being a strongman. And I promised her I'd finish top three at Britain's Strongest Man in January and be World's Strongest Man within the next three years. Sinead didn't look convinced, but she saw that my mind was made up.

I then went on Facebook and made my promise public. And as well as winning World's Strongest Man for Sinead, I said I'd do it as a tribute to Mum. Once I'd done that, I didn't really have a choice but to make it happen.

● ● ●

A key thing Dan taught me was that every strongman has different body mechanics, which means every strongman has to do things his own way. We're all different heights, with different-length arms and legs, different-sized hands and feet. So, while Luke's got one of the best squat forms in the world, I can't squat like him, because he's five inches shorter than me. I'm one of the best deadlifters in the world, but my deadlift technique would be wrong for Luke.

Another coach might look at my deadlift technique and say, 'Your back's too round.' But Dan understood that just because my technique wasn't textbook, and would have been wrong for someone else, that didn't mean it was wrong for me. Some people still think I lift Atlas Stones wrong. They'll look at me and think, 'How the hell is he not in hospital?' because they've probably been taught to lift stuff with a perfectly straight back. They don't understand I haven't always lifted Atlas Stones like that – I've built up my body to be able to withstand lifting them that way. What's dangerous for other people can be perfectly safe for strongmen, because we prac-tise so much and understand our bodies so well.

It was Dan who persuaded me to develop a 'power belly', which are those massive guts strongmen have. He said to me, 'I guarantee you you'll win World's Strongest Man with one.' But when I started doing strongman, I was adamant I'd never have a power belly. I remember saying to Luke, 'I don't want to be one of those fat strongmen. I want to be like Mariusz Pudzianowski or Derek Poundstone – strong as a monster but with a superhero's body.' So, for quite a few years, I didn't have a power belly, I had a six-pack instead.

Under a T-shirt, power bellies can look like beer guts. But while there's a lot of fat in a power belly, because of all the food strongmen have to eat, there's also a lot of muscle. That means power bellies don't wobble, like a beer gut – they're rock solid. But when I started developing my power belly, I didn't like it at all.

Suddenly, I couldn't see my abs, which I'd worked so hard to get. I thought people must be looking at me and thinking, 'Jesus, he must put away a lot of beer and takeaways.' But I eventually understood the power belly's importance.

While bodybuilders try to get as lean as they possibly can, so all their muscles and veins are popping out, lots of strongmen opt for a layer of fat to protect their muscles and joints, otherwise they'd wreck themselves. If a bodybuilder tried lifting an Atlas Stone they'd snap their biceps, because they don't have that same protection. As for a power belly, it can take a lot more pressure off the back than abs can. It gives a strongman an extremely strong core, which enables him to lift ludicrously heavy things without injuring himself.

You do have to be a bit careful with power bellies. Some strongmen's bellies are very extreme, which is great if you want to rest something on there, like a log. But they can be a problem when picking stuff up, like stones or sandbags, because they get in the way and make it more difficult to bend down. As with any elite sport, the line between getting things right and getting things wrong is fine, and it can be the difference between triumph and disaster.

After winning Scotland's Strongest Man for the first time, it was a case of, 'Right, I'm now the strongest man in my own country, what's next?' I didn't let it go to my head, partly because I'd seen what a bit of success had done to Luke. By his own admission, Luke got a bit cocky when he started winning competitions.

When Luke started competing in bigger competitions, he soon realised he was a small fish in a big pond. I think that's when he thought, 'Wow, I'm not actually that good. I need to show more respect to my competitors.' Once again, I was able to learn from Luke's mistakes. But winning Scotland's Strongest Man did make me a lot more confident in my own ability. Before, it was other people saying how much they believed in me. Now, I truly believed in myself, which is far more important. I was putting in the work and being rewarded. And I loved that feeling of winning and wanted it again and again.

Compared to Luke, I had it easy. When Luke started strongman, he was flying blind. He had no-one telling him what to do, had hardly any equipment and would often have to make do with whatever heavy stuff was lying around. Even when I started out, we had that stone with the sharp edges and sandbags that would burst open every time we tried to lift them.

I'd sometimes think, 'Jeez, am I doing the right sport?' But in hindsight, I think living in the middle of nowhere and having to seek stuff out made us more industrious and mentally stronger than strongmen from big towns and cities, who had all the best facilities and equipment on their doorstep. A bit like Opa, when he had to get on his bike and look for work, because he knew nothing was going to come to him.

As time went on, and we started to make our names in strongman, we started building up a proper collection of strongman equipment. When people see some of the stuff we've got now, they can't believe it. We have welders and joiners sending us stuff out of the blue. A guy from Ireland even carved us a beautiful big yoke and sent it over on the ferry. But being up in the Highlands means we still have to do things differently to strongmen from big towns and cities. For example, we'll take dips in the North Sea, and no-one in their right mind would do that. But it keeps us tougher than the average strongman.

I also had people like Eddie Hall giving me advice when I first arrived on the scene. Eddie was particularly generous, giving me tips and teaching me tricks, which he didn't have to do. Even after I bombed at Britain's Strongest Man in 2018, Eddie kept the faith and told me I was still going to be the best one day.

Eddie retired after winning his fifth straight British title in 2018, but he's never stopped supporting me. Eddie's son has ADHD, so he loves the fact that someone like me is succeeding, demonstrating that people with neurodevelopment disorders can do great things in life. It's very humbling to think that someone like Eddie, a true strongman great, is inspired by me.

With 'The Beast' out of the way, I thought I had a chance of winning Britain's Strongest Man in 2019. I had to finish in the top three, otherwise Sinead would have killed me. But things weren't looking good after the frame carry, the second event. The frame weighed 400kg and we had to carry it 20 metres in 60 seconds. But I only managed to carry it six metres and was the only man in the field who didn't reach the finish line. You need a very strong grip to be good at the frame carry, and grip events were my Achilles heel back then. As soon as my hands started getting sore, I'd drop whatever I was holding. But I suspected it was in the mind, rather than something physical.

I fell even further behind after the deadlift, despite doing nine reps of 320kg, and needed a grandstand finish to make the podium and fulfil my promise to Sinead. Luckily, I managed to pull one out. I won the loading race (2 x 125kg sacks, 2 x 150kg kegs, 1 x 115kg tyre), beating Luke into second place, before blitzing the field in the Atlas Stones.

I'd already made a name for myself in the stones – it just came naturally to me. But just because you're 6ft 8in with long levers, that doesn't mean you're going to be able to pick up massive stones. There's a lot of technique involved and it's a whole-body workout. And there's one exercise I do in training I know no other strongman does. I'm not giving anything away, but I'm convinced that's what takes me to another level.

That day, I did five stones in 18 seconds, more than three seconds faster than the next man. And my late surge secured third place, just a few points ahead of Luke. Graham Hicks won the title, his first, with his old rival Adam Bishop finishing second. But Eddie, who was commentating for TV, said I was his natural successor – 'The next Beast.' That was lovely to hear.

I was the first Scotsman to finish in the top three for 17 years. I'd beaten the likes of Laurence Shahlaei and Terry Hollands, former champions and legends of the sport. Standing up there on the podium, I finally felt like I deserved to be there and truly belonged. Jeez, it felt good. I only wished Mum had been there to see it.

It's amazing what you can achieve if you believe in yourself, stop worrying what anyone else thinks and commit to something 100 per cent. I left Sheffield thinking, 'I'm still only 24 and I've just come third in Britain on a month of full-time training. What could I do with another year under my belt?'

A few months later, I was in Leeds for my first Europe's Strongest Man. While Britain's Strongest Man has been won by some big names, Europe's Strongest Man has been won by some of the all-time greats, including five-time world champion Mariusz Pudzianowski and four-time world champions Jón Páll Sigmarsson, Magnús Ver Magnússon and Žydrūnas Savickas.

Thor Björnsson, a three-time winner, came into the event as the world's strongest man, having won his first title in Manila the previous year. Also competing was Poland's Mateusz Kieliszkowski, who had finished second behind Thor in Manila. Mateusz got off to a flying start in the log press, pulling out 214kg to my 190kg. I finished mid-pack in the deadlift for reps, and third in the flip and drag, which required us to flip over massive tyres and pull giant anchors. But then my Achilles heel flared up again, this time in the Hercules hold, a new event for me.

The Hercules hold consists of two massive weights, usually pillars, attached to chains. The athlete stands between the pillars and grabs the handles, before the pillars are released. As you can imagine, most people would let go immediately. But Mark Felix managed to hang on for 82 seconds, 25 seconds longer than the next man. Mark's fingers must be made of tungsten. Meanwhile, I was only able to hang on for 31 seconds, which meant I finished last in the event and tumbled down the overall standings.

Luke and I went head-to-head in the Atlas Stones, which was emotional. I finished in just under 22 seconds, before running over to Luke and roaring encouragement. I didn't think Luke was going to lift that last stone, which weighed 200kg, but with me going mental at him, he managed it. As you can imagine, the crowd lapped that up. Dad must have been in bits.

Having finished fourth and sixth respectively in Leeds, Luke and I had five months to prepare for World's Strongest Man in Bradenton, Florida. And this time we had a brand spanking new gym to train in. Our old garage had served a purpose, but it was very basic and not particularly inviting for other people who wanted to train with us. So along with his business partner Stacey Brown, who's a fitness coach, Luke opened a gym in a former tyre garage on an industrial estate. It was only a couple of basic units to start out with, but it felt more professional.

Florida's a bit different to Invergordon. For starters, Bradenton sits on a long white beach and is screamingly hot in June. But to succeed in strongman, you have to be versatile. This time my goal was to progress from my heat and reach the finals. If Luke could join me there, even better.

All the big names were there, minus Big Z, who had pulled out injured. But the competition was blown wide open on the first day when Thor, the reigning champion and red-hot favourite, tore a muscle in his foot. Carrying two 150kg weights, followed by a 450kg yoke, followed by a 600kg yoke, over a course of 21 metres will do that to you.

Thor still won his heat, but Luke kept his side of the Stoltman bargain, finishing second to reach the finals for the first time. Then it was my turn. My competition kicked off with the truck pull – the truck weighing 11 tonnes. The truck pull is probably the most recognised event in strongman, because it looks so mad – how on earth can a man pull an 11-tonne truck? Or a fire engine? Or even a plane? People just can't get their heads around it.

Obviously, the harness helps. And we usually have a rope to pull on. But it's one of the most agonising events in strongman, because every muscle in your body is working to its maximum. The hardest part of any vehicle pull is getting it moving. And if you lose momentum, it's almost impossible to restart.

As a rule, heavier strongmen are better at pulling vehicles, simply because mass moves mass. But Mariusz Pudzianowski was pretty handy at pulling vehicles, and he was relatively small. Technique is key: you want to stay as low as possible, your body almost parallel to the ground. The lower you are, the more force you can exert through your legs and hips. That's why we prepare with thousands of squats in the gym.

But training for a vehicle pull isn't just about lifting heavy, we also need to be doing lots of reps, because the event requires you to take lots of steps. Most strongmen will use a prowler – that pushing machine you see in gyms – to hone their body position, and a drag sled attached to a rope to improve their pulling skills. But if you've got an actual truck to practise with, all the better.

In Bradenton, we were supposed to pull the truck 22 metres in 75 seconds, but after a few strides my heart was almost coming out of my chest and I felt like I was on fire, what with all the lactic acid coursing through my body. As a result, I fell inches short of the finish line, which was a disappointing start. How Thor managed to complete the course in 34 seconds – before his injury, to be fair – is anyone's guess.

I got back on track with second place in the giant's medley, the event that nobbled Thor. And I also grabbed joint second in the deadlift, which required us to rep a couple of cars weighing 375kg in total. I managed eight, one less than American Martins Licis, who was looking like a title contender. I was third after the overhead log press, which saw me push out five reps of 155kg in 75 seconds and meant that I qualified for the finals with my big brother. We were the first brothers in history to do that, which was mind-blowing. Now it was about having some fun in the Florida sun.

Even a year earlier, the idea that I'd go out and enjoy myself in a World's Strongest Man finals would have been ridiculous. I still felt like an imposter in that kind of company and my mind was weak. But something had drastically changed since my breakdown at Britain's Strongest Man. Since becoming a full-time strongman, I'd felt more secure. I was a professional, with the best coach in the world. I had a big brother beside me every step of the way. We even had our own gym. I belonged in that kind of company because I'd made it that way.

There were lots of great names in the finals, lads who'd been on the circuit for years. Brian Shaw was appearing in his eleventh, Thor in his ninth and Canada's JF Caron in his seventh. There was also Mateusz Kieliszkowski, who'd finished second the previous year, and Georgia's Konstantine Janashia, who was appearing in his fourth finals. And then there was Martins Licis, who'd finished second behind Thor at the recent Arnold Strongman Classic, the prestigious strength event created by Arnold Schwarzenegger.

Amazingly, I was leading them all after the first event, in which I managed to load a 120kg barrel, a 140kg anvil and two 140kg sacks onto a platform in just under 40 seconds. Oh, I almost forgot, we had to carry each item 12 metres – on sand. The organisers are always finding ways to make things harder for us. I finished sixth in the overhead medley – two 60kg dumbbells, one 100kg circus dumbbell, one 160kg barbell and a 170kg log – but well down the field in the squat lift and the deadlift hold.

Heading into the Atlas Stones, I had no chance of making the podium. But I put in a decent performance, finishing third in that event. This meant I finished fifth overall, 16 points behind new champion Martins Licis, but two places ahead of Luke and one place ahead of Brian Shaw, one of the all-time greats and a huge hero of mine.

That competition changed it all. I'd come fifth while enjoying the experience. I'd finished higher than any Scotsman in history. I'd blown everyone out of the water in one of the events. I thought, 'Well, all that stuff must mean something.' And probably for the first time, I truly believed I could be the best in the world.

9

INTERLUDE

DAN HIPKISS

Our wonderful mum.
Us back in the 90s.

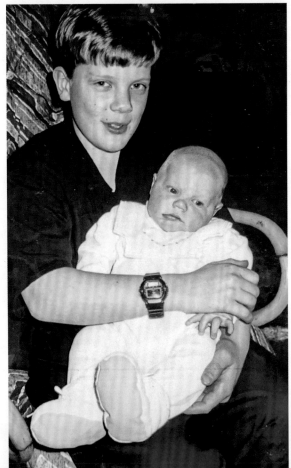

An early pic with baby Tom.

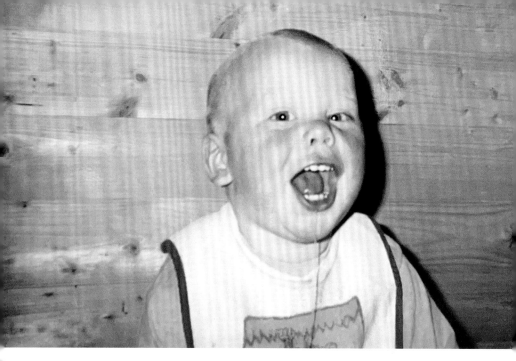

Baby Tom!

All the siblings:
Luke, Nikki, Jodie,
Tom and Harry.

Tom and Harry playing around in our garden.

Making the most of that lovely Scottish weather.

Tom's early forays into stone lifting with Dad and Jodie.

Luke and Mum back in the day.

Tom and Mum:
always inseparable.

Showing Tom the ropes
from a young age!

Note the retro Gameboy here!

Tom and Mum at Tom's engagement party.

The beginnings of our interest in Strongman … Luke channelling our Opa's incredible strength.

Opa in action.

Tom and Mum.

Baby-faced first steps
into Strongman.

I am Luke and Tom's coach and I've been with them since 2019. I tried being a strongman myself but wasn't very good at it. I did a coaching qualification at Sheffield Hallam University, where I trained with the weightlifting team, coaching some of their individual athletes. One of the guys, Paul Smith, had been competing in strongman for about four or five years, and he invited me along to a competition. I gave him some advice, he ended up winning and suddenly I was a strongman coach.

The first time I met Tom was at UK's Strongest Man in 2017. He was just about the perfect physical specimen, but mentally he was nowhere near where he needed to be. You could beat Tom before a competition started.

Tom and I hit it off, and I wasn't afraid to tell him what I really thought. When he finished fifth at World's Strongest Man in Florida in 2019, I told him he should have won it. Scotland's Strongest Man was a few months later, so I said to Tom, 'I'll coach you for free until then. If it works, we'll carry on. If it doesn't, we won't.' He won Scotland's Strongest Man, pulled a massive personal best in the deadlift and we've been stuck with each other since then.

An issue with a lot of elite-level athletes is that they're treated with too much reverence. Tom was pulling a 400kg in the deadlift, which is pretty big. But it wasn't the deadlift that would help win him World's Strongest Man. In essence, Tom was being told he was great when he was actually just very good.

My coaching is based around weakness. It's not much fun for my athletes, because they spend a lot of time feeling rubbish about themselves. But they're never going to improve enough to compete on the biggest stage if they focus on stuff they're good at. And as a competition gets closer, they start to realise the stuff that used to be a struggle isn't a struggle anymore.

When Luke saw the results Tom was getting with me as his coach, he started to take notice. Eventually, Luke decided to come on board as well. But I certainly don't train them the same. You can't have a blanket approach, because everyone is different.

Because Tom is autistic and has always been guided by people, most of the time I can just tell him what he needs to do, without having to explain it. However, there are times he'll want us to have a chat and work something out together. It's about what makes him happy, because if he's not happy, he won't train as well. Luke, on the other hand, has always been very self-sufficient and has spent a lot of his time guiding Tom. For that reason, he was more reluctant to let me in. We're mostly over that bridge now, but it's still more of a two-way conversation, because he likes to know why he's doing what he's doing.

Family time is very important for both of them, so I quickly realised we had to make strongman a job. Typically, they train Monday to Fridays and have weekends off. If they didn't have those weekends off, they'd get stressed. And when you get stressed, a hormone called cortisol is released, a response to stress which keeps you in a state of fight or flight. If you have too much cortisol in your system over time, it can cause problems.

A lot of athletes think that the more hours they spend training, the better they'll be. But it's pointless doing too much. If you were training for a marathon, you wouldn't run a marathon every day, otherwise your body would be in pieces by the day of the race. In the same way, an intense but relatively short session in the gym is normally enough for a strongman (although event-specific training can take 3 – 5 hours). The quicker you can get the practice work done in the gym, the better. Because if a session that used to take two hours now takes an hour and a half, you're half an hour fitter. I'm a big fan of a mountaineer called Nims Purja, and he always says that sometimes when you feel like you are knackered, you're actually only about 45 per cent knackered. So it's about getting Tom and Luke to understand that even if they don't feel 100 per cent, they still feel good enough to get a session done.

Generally, people are quite lazy and want training to feel nice and comfortable. And Tom and Luke used to do a set of exercises each and then sit and chat for a while. Now, they'll do their sets back-to-back, without any breaks. They've adapted to being uncomfortable and it's made them fitter.

Tom and Luke sometimes call some of my methods 'weird hippy nonsense', but to me it's mostly common sense. I see Tom and Luke as strength athletes, rather than strongmen. They're not powerlifters, who just stand in one spot and lift, they have to be able to move as well. So, I'll often say to Tom and Luke, 'Loading medleys are won when you're not carrying something.' The person who wins a moving event isn't necessarily the strongest, he's the person who can retrieve each item and pick it up the quickest. That's why conditioning is so important in strongman.

If it's a one-day competition, like most of them are, there'll be five or six events in four or five hours. Obviously, competitors have to be brutally strong, but you'll see so many athletes perform great in the first couple of events before their conditioning lets them down. Not Tom. At the Rogue Invitational in 2021, he did one of the events before going for a run, because he still had some energy left. Meanwhile, other guys were flat on their backs taking in oxygen.

Strongmen are massive, so just existing is fairly hard work. But Tom and Luke are fit enough for their sport. In fact, I'd say they're two of the healthiest strongmen on the circuit. They do more cardio and conditioning work than most seem to, and since their nutritionist Nathan Payton has come on board, their diets have been perfect. They get regular health checks, because they don't just want longevity in strongman, they want longevity in life. It doesn't matter if you win World's Strongest Man if you're going to die in your forties or fifties.

Aspiring strongmen often ask me what books they should read or what podcasts they should listen to. To be honest, I can't think of anything worse than reading or listening to strongman coaches talking about their methods. Don't get me wrong, I enjoy watching old strongman competitions. But I'm more interested in watching other sports and seeing what we can learn from them.

American footballers get paid millions of dollars a year to do what they do, which often involves covering short distances ridiculously fast. So it makes sense for strongmen to train like they do. During Tom and Luke's general physical preparedness phase, when they're not lifting very heavy weights, I try to get them more athletic in one short block. That means doing lots of shuttle runs and cone drills like American footballers do.

I've also had a longstanding interest in Parkour, which involves getting from point A to point B as quickly as possible. Parkour athletes are good at pretty much everything – running, climbing, swinging, rolling, crawling – and if they can't jump very well, they'll either badly injure themselves or die. Strongman doesn't involve much jumping, but jumping is one of the most explosive movements a human can do. So, I found out what made Parkour athletes so good at it, before introducing it to Tom and Luke's training. They hated it at first. But after a few months, Luke said all that jumping had improved his overall movement.

Just as strongmen can learn from what other athletes do in training, they can also learn about the mind. Usually, successful sportspeople could have been successful in lots of other sports. Tiger Woods chose golf, but with his physical attributes and mental strength, it probably could have been anything. If Michael Jordan had discovered tennis as a kid, rather than basketball, who knows how many Grand Slams he would have won. The activity is secondary – it's what's inside the person that makes them great.

Genetics is obviously important when it comes to strong-man. Tom's 6ft 8in with a positive wingspan, which is pretty much perfect when it comes to lifting stones and whatever else. But there are countless people with good genetics who spend most of their time in the pub. And there are lots of other genetically gifted people who spend most of their time in the gym but whose minds prevent them from making it as an athlete. So, it would be mad to look at Tom and think, 'Of course he's the World's Strongest Man, look at the size of him.' He only became World's Strongest Man because of his mind and hard work.

It's taken Tom a lot of work to get his mind right. And it can still get stronger. Take the Hercules hold. He's really good at it in training – his grip strength is actually amazing. But he's convinced himself it's a bad event for him, which means he usually underperforms in competitions. That's where his concrete thinking, which is usually so helpful, is a problem. There's always this little voice in his head telling him to let go. But we also had issues with the dumbbell before I got him to use a different dumbbell of the same weight and he smashed it. Suddenly, it wasn't a bad event for him. So, I reckon if he has one good Hercules hold in competition, that will change everything.

Up to a point, the heavier you are, the more weight you can move. For Tom, being as big as possible at a competition is a psychological boost, but it took a bit of persuading to get him to develop a power belly. However, it's not healthy walking around at competition weight all year round, so you can often see his abs instead. But when he arrives at World's Strongest Man, and just eats and sleeps for four or five days, he gets noticeably bigger. Because he feels big, he feels strong. And because he feels strong, he feels confident. But smaller guys do sometimes prevail in strongman, and always because they're more technical and professional than everyone else.

The best example is Finland's Jouko Ahola. Ahola was only 6ft 1in and about 125kg, so he shouldn't have come anywhere near to winning World's Strongest Man. But he won it twice, in 1997 and 1999. That's because he'd do stuff like marking handles and making sure his runway was the cleanest in the moving events. Ukraine's Oleksii Novikov would be his modern equivalent.

But Tom and Luke don't think like they do. Probably because they're so naturally big and strong, they've never needed to. That's why I insist on being at as many competitions as possible, so I can do the thinking for them. I'm big into motorsport and rock climbing, both sports where attention to detail is key to performance. And I try to channel my attention to detail into Tom and Luke. It's usually a case of just telling them what to do before an event. But I'd like them to get to the stage where they can marry their natural talent with their own nerdy perfectionism, and I can take a step back.

Nathan, Amy (the lads' psychologist) and I are very joined up. During the build-up to a major competition, I'll speak to Amy every week. Their sessions with Amy are obviously very personal, but they've given her permission to pass on anything I need to know from a coaching point of view. I'm also in regular contact with Nathan, who's the best in the world at what he does. If Tom or Luke message me and say, 'I didn't feel good in the gym today', I'll talk to Nathan about their diet and we'll adapt their training. Generally, it's a case of feeding them until they feel better. But Nathan might want them on a 'low diet' for a couple of weeks, to reset everything. And I need to know if that's happening, so I don't push them too hard and they end up getting injured.

Strongman is fundamentally dangerous. But I spend my spare time rock climbing and racing cars, so I know all about making risky things as safe as possible.

I'm often asked how much stronger people can get. It's impossible to say, but supposedly impossible records get broken all the time. Fourteen years ago, four people in the world had deadlifted 400kg. Now, people are doing 400kg for reps. And at Giants Live competitions, there might be ten guys pulling over 450kg.

What I will say is that the rate of progression will slow. When Eddie Hall deadlifted 500kg, he broke the world record by 35kg. As a percentage increase, that's the equivalent of someone running the 100m in 7.5 seconds. I'm not sure something like that will happen again. But there will always be progression, especially if more people start taking up strongman. Maybe there are guys out there with the potential to lift 550kg, but they'll never know it unless they try the sport.

As for Tom and Luke, it's hard to tell how much higher they can go. Dealing in numbers is often pointless, because if you can win a deadlift with 450kg, then why bother almost killing yourself to lift 500kg? And numbers on a bar mean nothing next to winning shiny things. Tom could end up winning six world titles, which would make him the greatest strongman ever.

Luke has been very focused on business and family, and his training hasn't always been as good as it could have been. He was dominant in the group stage at World's Strongest Man in 2022 but tailed off in the finals. But his journey is nowhere near done. The only people who want him to win World's Strongest Man more than he does himself are me and Tom. Even to see him up there on the podium would mean as much to me as one of Tom's titles. If Luke can have a perfect preparation, there's no reason why he can't win one.

I saw the potential in Tom and told him he'd win World's Strongest Man. But he still had to go out and do it, which meant holding himself to certain standards. And that's not something I've always done myself. My past is chequered, that's how most people describe it. I used to exist week to week, rather than planning for a better future. I suppose you could say I was a bit of a mess-up. But that's the beauty of our working relationship – I might be their coach, but they've taught me so much more. And the main lesson I've learned is that when you've got your stuff together, and you back yourself, you can achieve crazy things in life.

10

FULL-TIME RESULTS

LUKE

Typically, Tom's gone galloping ahead with his story, so let's get you up to speed with what was going on with me. A week after Europe's Strongest Man in 2016, I won Scotland's Strongest Man for the fourth year straight. A couple of months later, it was time for my first World's Strongest Man in Botswana. I was delighted to get the invite.

Unfortunately, my preparations weren't exactly elite. I'd only recently moved back from South Korea, just had a new house built and got married, and Mum was terminally ill. On top of that, I got stuck on an oil rig after a three-week stint. I was due to leave on the Friday and fly out to Botswana the following Tuesday. But some bad weather came in, as often happens in the North Sea, and I couldn't escape until the Tuesday morning.

That was one of the most stressful days of my life. My flight was changed, so I had to go to Aberdeen instead of Inverness. That meant I couldn't go home, because I didn't have time. Kushi wasn't able to join but she packed my bag for me and gave it to a mate who was accompanying me to the competition. I arrived at Heathrow carrying my offshore bag and still wearing my offshore clothes. When I got on the plane to

Johannesburg, I must have been stinking to high heaven. To whoever was sitting anywhere near me, I can only say sorry.

After arriving in Johannesburg, from where we were flying on to Kasane, I descended an escalator and first laid eyes on the opposition. It was like entering the land of the giants. I'd done a lot of competitions by then, but this was ridiculous. And it wasn't just Thor and Brian Shaw, who must have weighed 800lb between them, it was the whole gang.

Because most of them had been on the strongman scene for longer than me, they oozed confidence. Just the way they carried themselves – heads up, arms swinging – made them seem even bigger. They were also decked out in the best gear and covered in sponsors, while I was wearing some tatty tracksuit bottoms and a smelly old T-shirt. At that moment, everything felt completely unattainable.

You don't infiltrate a group like that straightaway. Especially if you smell like a tramp. I was the new guy on the block and the old hands were there to do a job. As professional athletes, they weren't really interested in making new friends or doling out advice – they were interested in winning.

I was in a heat with three former finalists, including England's Mark Felix. Mark is an absolute freak, in the nicest possible way. A year after taking up strongman in his mid-thirties, he was competing in World's Strongest Man. In 2006, at the age of 40, he finished fourth. Most people would have thought, 'Right, that's me done, there's no way I'm gonna get any better in middle age.' But Mark just kept getting stronger. At World's Strongest Man in 2016, he was 50. And he's still competing at the time of writing! They don't call him 'The Miracle' for nothing. Who knows what Mark could have achieved if he'd gone full-time. He's stayed impressively grounded despite his success, even keeping up his job as a plasterer.

I found Mark incredibly inspiring. I'd taken up strongman relatively late, but a man competing with the elite at the age of 50 was just insane. I just don't know how anyone can put their body through so much for so long. Most 50-year-olds would struggle to do ten press-ups, but Mark's grip strength was still world-class in 2016, as was his deadlift. Mark wasn't in Botswana to make up the numbers – he really believed he could become World's Strongest Man.

Whenever he's interviewed, Mark says he's never going to retire from strongman. I believe him, because he loves it so much, and I know how addictive the buzz that comes from competing is. I don't think I'll still be competing in my mid-fifties, though. For a start, Kushi wouldn't put up with it. But Mark at least shows it's possible. He's a bona fide legend of the sport.

What I also learned from Mark is that you don't have to be an arrogant fool, always shouting and showing off, to thrive in strongman. He's the nicest guy you could meet, a proper gentleman. Sometimes the lads will be effing and blinding and Mark will say, 'Man, you shouldn't be saying stuff like that.' And because he's such a hero, and so respected, we do as we're told.

Mark and I finished joint third in our heat, which meant we missed out on the finals. I was frustrated with that, but proud at the same time. I'd finished mid-pack in all the events and proved a lot of people wrong. When my competitors first saw me in Johannesburg, they must have wondered what the cat had dragged in. But far from disgracing myself, I'd proved I belonged.

Not that I had much time to dwell on my performance, because as soon as I got home from Botswana, I had to head offshore again. My life was constantly swinging between love and hate, passion and indifference. And I knew working offshore meant I wasn't living up to my potential as a strongman. But instead of doing something about it, I continued stewing.

We were back in Botswana for World's Strongest Man in 2017, this time in the capital Gaborone, about ten miles from the border with South Africa. And somehow, I found myself in an even tougher heat than the year before.

As well as Martins Licis, who'd topped our heat in Kasane, I was up against Thor, the reigning European champion. As expected, Thor romped through to the finals, winning three of the five qualifying events, but I pushed Martins all the way. If I'd won the final event, which involved tossing gold bullion over a five-metre bar, I'd have finished joint second overall. As it was, Iceland's Stefán Pétursson took first, meaning I finished one point behind Martins and was eliminated. I was getting closer to the finals, but something was still missing.

• • •

With Mum no longer around, I started making more of a racket when Tom was competing. I've got a deep, booming voice, and I knew it intimidated other athletes. It even intimidated Tom at first. I remember him saying to me, 'You're scaring me shouting like that!' But I kept getting louder, because I knew Tom needed someone to listen to, someone to guide him, someone to fill him with confidence. I needed him to know it was okay to go all out. Because I knew that would make him unbeatable.

But back in 2017, Tom was still very wet behind the ears. And I actually think I put him under too much pressure. I'd speak about Tom a lot, about how strong he was and how great he was going to be. And when Eddie Hall started saying the same things, Tom found that difficult to cope with.

He was still new to a senior competition environment, and would still get nervous the night before. If someone wanted to interview him, I'd usually sit in, to elaborate on his yes and no answers. I was like a comfort blanket, putting him more at ease, making sure he didn't have to think too much.

Tom went into Britain's Strongest Man in 2018 thinking he was going to win it. He was very outspoken on social media and I actually said to him, 'Stop putting so much pressure on yourself. Take a step back and just worry about doing the best you can.' All that stuff Eddie was saying about him had gone to his head, and he seemed to have forgotten about his iffy shoulder. Then he went and finished last. It was very tough for him to take.

But there are two ways to deal with failure: either you let it destroy you or you learn from it and become stronger, in mind and body. As it was, after a prolonged break, Tom returned even more determined than he was before. Luckily, Tom's calamity had a positive effect on me as well.

I'd seen what complacency had done to Tom. He'd become too comfortable and too blasé. He assumed that because he was improving in the gym, he'd win the events in competition. He didn't consider that his competitors were also grafting like maniacs and improving too. I was determined not to fall into the same trap, and that was one of the beauties of our partnership: if something happened to one of us, positive or negative, we both learned from it and improved as a result.

My day job meant I only competed once in 12 months after my outing in Gaborone, finishing sixth at Britain's Strongest Man, a country mile behind the winner Eddie Hall. And in May 2018, I once again just failed to make it out of my heat at World's Strongest Man in Manila, losing in a stone-off to Johan Els, the strongest man in Africa. I'll be honest, these near misses were starting to get quite irritating.

I almost didn't even make it as far as the stone-off, because the bus pull that year was hell. Pulling a bus, truck or plane is hard. Luckily, I knew a few drivers, and they'd sometimes let me and Tom pull their lorry across an industrial estate in Invergordon. However, when you do a pull event in a competition, the organisers will always put a little hill at the end of the course. They're not nice people. Having built a nice bit of momentum over the flat part of the course, which is a beautiful feeling, hitting that hill feels like suddenly being whacked in the face with a cricket bat. But if you manage to finish, you feel euphoric.

We all expected the bus pull in Manila to be horrible, but the heat and humidity made it outright dangerous. They had us waiting in a tent for five or six hours, and it wasn't air-conditioned as promised. Pulling this 13-tonne bus, I was literally shaking. Every tug on the rope was 100 per cent output and doing that for 40-odd seconds in those conditions will hollow you out. Everyone was blowing up, and when I finished, they had to cover me with ice to cool me down. I never wanted to see another bus after that, not even the 25A from Invergordon to Inverness.

Later that year, Tom brought my five-year reign as Scotland's Strongest Man to an end. He probably would have beaten me before then, had I not been his older brother. But once he'd cleared that psychological blockage, it was inevitable.

That said, I did get a big slice of bad luck in the truck pull. It was arm over arm, meaning we were pulling the truck while sat on the floor, with our legs pushing against a block. It was me against Tom, and I thought I had a decent chance of beating him. But when the whistle went, Tom's truck started flying towards us, while mine was barely moving. There was no give in the rope, and I honestly thought someone might have left the handbrake on. Tom finished in 20-odd seconds, but I didn't finish in time. Tom still probably would have won the title, but I was very annoyed I'd lost my title in that fashion.

● ● ●

Tom's right, he was a different beast in 2019. But so was I. In my first few years of strongman, things were always a bit hit and miss. But I learned from every competition and was starting to feel more in control.

Whenever you start competing in something, you naturally take your cues from more experienced rivals. That can work when it comes to stuff like mental preparation, but not when it comes to the technicalities of lifting and moving. Tom's a lot bigger than me, with longer arms and legs, so we do things differently. Eddie Hall is one of the best deadlifters ever, but I couldn't replicate his technique, because our bodies aren't the same. I needed to focus on myself and work out what was best for me. And, after a couple of years, I was going into competitions with a lot more confidence, knowing that if I lifted a certain weight or posted a certain time, I'd score well.

Away from the actual competing, I'd felt at home in strongman since the early days. In that kind of environment, there are big personalities and shrinking violets; people who make a lot of noise and people who don't say much; people who are constantly winding people up and people who are the butt of most of the jokes. But I'd spent so much time on the rigs, especially in tea shacks all over the world, I was already used to all that daftness. I had a hatful of comebacks if the banter was flying. I knew what it was like to be hollered at by some mad scaffolder. I knew what to say when someone was telling me some ridiculous story, like the time some wee guy told me he was a major drug dealer and the boat we could see coming in to shore was full of his gear. I called him an idiot and laughed in his face. Because of that grounding, Eddie Hall acting up during a rules meeting wasn't going to faze me.

Tom and I finished third and fourth respectively at Britain's Strongest Man in 2019 – the first time he'd beaten me in that competition – before we both headed to Florida for another crack at World's Strongest Man. And when we became the first set of brothers to qualify for the finals, it proved we were virtually operating as a single entity, instead of two separate people.

The biggest change happened when we opened our own gym in the spring of 2019. As Tom mentioned, we went from training on gravel in my garage to training in a couple of spacious units, with concrete under our feet. Nothing was said between us, but that's when Tom and I really started to push things to another level. Having made that investment in ourselves, we had to step up. We didn't really have a choice.

On the flip side, I wasn't able to use my own gym for great chunks of the year, because I was still working offshore. And because the offshore gyms usually didn't have much weight in them, I'd end up doing muscular endurance, involving lots of high reps. When I got back to Invergordon, I'd go really heavy again. But I might only be home for three or four days before I'd get another job offer, which I'd have to take. Then I'd be offshore for another few weeks, in some terrible gym, back to doing muscular endurance. There was no point having a plan, because it was impossible for me to follow one.

When I was offshore, I'd watch social media videos of rival strongmen – the likes of Thor and Brian Shaw – lifting in their plush gyms and feel so frustrated. Then I'd head to the gym and spend an hour bouncing around on a treadmill, thinking, 'I'm stuck in the middle of the North Sea, running on the spot while my competitors are preparing properly. This is awful.'

I was also becoming more aware of the toxicity that sometimes came with offshore life. When you're away for weeks at a time, you need a partner you can trust 100 per cent. I had that in Kushi, but I know other people who weren't so lucky. They'd discover the bad news when they got home, return offshore in terrible shape and self-destruct.

There can also be quite a bit of back-stabbing on the rigs, because lots of guys are wanting to climb the career ladder. And because blokes mainly work offshore for the money – it's not always a great lifestyle choice – one-upmanship can be rife.

For a long time, I was caught up in that superficial world of conspicuous consumption. And I didn't realise what my time was worth. I looked at the money I was making and thought, 'Well, it means I can buy lots of nice things, so this is the way it has to be.' But towards the end, I realised none of that mattered. What's the point of earning a good salary when you're sitting on a rig for weeks at a time?

I remember being at home, sitting on the sofa in a pair of old tracksuit bottoms I'd bought for a tenner in Tesco. They had holes all over them and the waistband was frayed, but I didn't care. I was with my wife, and I was happy. It all comes down to time being the most valuable thing there is. But this realisation didn't make life any easier. It had the opposite effect. For three or four days before I went offshore, I'd be in a dark, resentful mood, which could sometimes cause problems with Kushi. And once I was out there, I'd be down in the dumps a lot of the time, desperately wanting to be elsewhere. But maybe I had to be as low as possible before I made any drastic changes.

One day, Colin Bryce, one of the owners of Giants Live, said to me, 'Luke, if you carry on doing strongman part-time, you'll carry on getting part-time results. You'll only get full-time results if you commit to it full-time.' Colin had been around the block and knew what he was talking about, so that really hit home.

Things came to a head in September 2019. Unlike the previous year, I was delighted when Tom pipped me to Scotland's Strongest Man. He was only a point ahead of me going into the final event, the Atlas Stones. And when he smashed me to retain his title, my overriding emotion was pride. Without meaning to sound patronising, that was when Tom came of age. This time, his big brother didn't have any excuses. I'd performed well, not made any stupid mistakes, and Tom had beaten me fair and square. It was what we both needed – a big confidence boost for Tom and a huge boot up the backside for me. The only problem being, while Tom was now a full-time strongman, I wasn't. If I didn't do something about it, Tom was going to leave me for dust.

After Scotland's Strongest Man, Tom was invited to Dubai to take part in an intensive training programme, ahead of a competition I was also taking part in. Tom was there for four weeks, with everything paid for. He even got to take Sinead with him. Meanwhile, I was stuck on a platform, doing just about the worst job there was. The gym was not only awful, but my bed was so small, about the width of a fish finger, that my shoulder was hanging over the side. One night, the lad in the bunk above me didn't stop snoring and it drove me absolutely nuts.

When I saw Tom's pictures of him and Sinead living it up in Dubai on social media, something changed inside me. I texted Kushi: 'I'm done. I'm not going offshore again. I hate this life. I need to do things that make me happy. I don't want to be one of those guys in the pub, going on about what he coulda, shoulda been. That would kill me. That's not who I am, not how I was brought up. I'm taking a risk, no doubt. But if I don't do it now, I'm never gonna do it.'

It wasn't nice for Kushi either, her husband being away for two or three weeks at a time. Before we got married, we thought that was just how it was going to be. That was my job, and I'd probably be doing it until I was 60-odd. But it didn't have to be like that. I had agency over my life.

I was a lead surveyor by then, doing alright for myself. But Kushi believed that whatever I did, I'd be successful. Most of all, she wanted me to be happy. And I was never happier than when I was in the gym.

A few weeks after that horrible job on a platform, I joined Tom in Dubai. And I beat him in the competition, finishing second to Tom's third. The prize money was pretty good. But it was about more than that. It was my best performance in an international event, and I felt proud as a result.

After being dethroned as Scotland's Strongest Man, I'd been relegated to 'Tom's big brother' in a lot of people's eyes. They thought I was past my best, would never achieve much in strongman, that there was now only one Stoltman in town.

That's why I was so pumped after beating Tom in Dubai. In fact, I ran towards the camera and called into the lens, 'Never count me out!' That was a nice moment.

I had one last random job onshore, just down the road from Invergordon. And I'll never forget leaving the job in my wee Renault Clio, which was tilted to one side because of an iffy suspension. I drove through the gates, pulled over as soon as I could, phoned Kushi and told her I was done.

I was free at last, heading into the unknown. I couldn't say how long I had left as a strongman or if the gym would ever make much money, but I was so incredibly happy, euphoric even. I cranked up the radio and grinned all the way home, before binning my boiler suit and the rest of my stinking gear.

Then I paid Dad a visit. He was delighted when I told him I'd quit. He'd spent far too long offshore as well, so knew exactly what it was doing to me. And he knew Mum wouldn't have wanted me doing a job I hated just for the salary, that she'd want me to take a chance and follow my passion. Seeing how happy Dad was for me, I knew I'd made the right decision. Full steam ahead.

11

TRAINING MY WEAKNESSES

TOM

I t's not as if it was all plain sailing after finishing fifth at World's Strongest Man in 2019. I was still a young man, and my body was still maturing. I was playing catch-up in certain events, because before I got Dan on board as coach, I didn't know how to train my weaknesses. He immediately got to work on my overhead lifts, squats and holds, but it took time for everything to come together.

A few weeks after World's Strongest Man in Florida, I finished ninth out of ten at a Giants Live competition at Wembley, before an eighth-place finish in Manchester a couple of months later. In both competitions, I blew up in the Hercules hold. But if I wanted to be the strongest man in the world, I couldn't make excuses.

With most competitions, including Britain's Strongest Man, they tell you the events a few months in advance, so you can concentrate on them in training. With World's Strongest Man, they only tell you the events a month or so beforehand, and they're vaguer. They'll tell you there's a loading event, but they won't tell you the implements. It's a guessing game, and you have to practise with every implement you have, all the way up to the competition. But whatever the events, there will always be some athletes happier than others. And if you have a weakness, you just have to practise harder at it.

I set a new Atlas Stones world record in Dubai, lifting ten of them, weighing between 100 and 200kg, in 40.7 seconds. Before I did that, I didn't think I'd be that bothered. But it gave me such a buzz, knowing I'd done something no human had ever done before. And I wanted to raise the record so high that no human would ever get close to it.

A few months later, I finished second at Britain's Strongest Man in Sheffield. It was very tight between me, Luke and Adam Bishop after three events, and the penultimate event was the Conan's wheel, which I'd never done before in competition. It's named after a scene in *Conan the Barbarian*, where slaves are pushing a massive wheel around as a punishment. And it's as brutal as it sounds.

The Conan's wheel required us to lift a frame carrying a 300kg quad bike and walk as far as possible in a circle. It's difficult to train specifically for the Conan's wheel, because you don't tend to see them in gyms, and good luck trying to build one. So, you just have to make sure you do plenty of endurance work, because otherwise you'd explode after a few steps. And it's also uncomfortable. You have to rest the bar on your forearms or in your elbow crease, and you essentially push with your diaphragm, which makes it difficult to breathe. No wonder strongmen sometimes collapse doing the Conan's wheel.

Adam Bishop turned the wheel 775 degrees to finish second in the event, and, while I didn't collapse, I only turned it 657 degrees to finish fourth, just behind Luke. I was a bit disappointed with that, and it meant I had to finish three spots ahead of Bish in the final event, the Atlas Stones, to win the trophy.

As it turned out, I set another new world record, lifting five stones in 16.01 seconds. But Bish was third, enough to finish half a point ahead of me and claim his first British title. Meanwhile, Luke was only three points behind me in third. I was disappointed not to have won, but I wasn't angry or depressed. I'd gone one better than last time, and was only one place from being the best in Britain, so I was heading in the right direction.

A few weeks earlier, I'd spent time with Eddie Hall, who'd taught me all about the importance of recovery. I already did recovery work, but Eddie made me realise I hadn't been giving it enough attention.

People assume strongmen are always injuring themselves lifting the weights we do, but we're more likely to injure ourselves doing something daft outside the gym, like the time I rolled my ankle playing football a week or so before World's Strongest Man. Or when Luke pulled a hamstring doing a sprint for a YouTube video. I've only had one strongman injury, the rotator cuff I tore at World's Strongest Man in 2017. And I was back in the gym two weeks later. That's because of the recovery work I do.

After a gym session, my body is broken down. And if I didn't do any recovery, I'd grind myself into dust over the course of a week. But with the right recovery, I'll reduce the 'doms' – delayed onset muscle soreness – which means I'll have an effective workout the following day. I could win a competition with one training day and six recovery days, but never the other way around. Without proper recovery, a strongman is like a sports car without regular maintenance.

A lot of people neglect their recovery because it can be quite boring. They've got no problem lifting weights all day, because that's the fun part, but they want to get out of the gym as soon as they're done. Mobility is as dull as it gets. When I first started doing it, I'd think, 'Why have I been stretching for an hour while everyone else is slamming weights on the floor?' But I soon realised that loads of people can lift massive weights, but by doing stuff other people didn't want to do I was gaining an edge. As any athlete will tell you, it's the boring stuff that makes the difference between success and failure.

All that stretching makes me much more flexible and balanced. That means I'm far less likely to injure myself when lifting, because I'm a lot looser and can maintain good form. I also have two hours of physio every week. That breaks the muscle down, gets all the knots and tightness out. A physio is like a mechanic, fiddling under the bonnet and tuning the engine. I also take hot and cold baths every day. I'd been doing this stuff before that meeting with Eddie, but I was now more religious about it, cutting no corners.

A lot of recovery is simply knowing when to rest, staying away from the gym if you feel too tired or sore. But that doesn't normally happen, because I've got everything else under control. Because I know I'm eating the right stuff and doing the right recovery, my body is essentially a machine, running without thinking and programmed to hit its peak before every competition.

The most important recovery I do is in the week before a competition. Before then, I'll be in the gym Monday to Thursday, trying to make things as tough as possible. That means that when I do my final events session on the Friday, my body will be battered. But after that, I'll put my feet up and spend the next few days eating, getting physio and not even thinking about strongman. By the Wednesday, I'll feel fresh as a daisy. And when the competition arrives, I'll be champing at the bit and my body will feel stronger than ever.

I'll see amateur strongmen posting videos of their workouts a couple of days before a competition, and then they can't understand why they don't perform. I think a lot of it comes down to fear. When I started out in strongman, I'd get scared I wasn't doing enough in the gym. When I failed to lift something, I'd think it was because I was weak. Then I'd put even more work in, thinking it would make me stronger. But it was overworking that was crashing my nervous system and making me fatigued. Or I might just have had an off day, which happens to everyone in all walks of life. Over time, I became confident enough to say, 'It doesn't matter that I'm not lifting enough weight in the gym. If I give my body a rest, I'll be able to do it in the competition.'

Other strongmen have to know for certain they can lift a certain weight before a competition. But before I set my Atlas Stone world record of 286kg, I hadn't gone near that weight in training. And I never go to my max in deadlift or log lift in the gym. It's no different to those experienced footballers you hear about who are pedestrian trainers but bang on the money on match day.

People sometimes ask me, 'Are strongmen actually healthy?' I suppose they see us as freakish, because of the things we lift, the amount we eat and the way we look, like ogres from some fantasy film. But my reply is always, 'Look at Mark Felix. He's in his mid-fifties and still competing at the highest level.'

If you met Mark, you wouldn't think he was a day over 40, and he's been competing for two decades and has appeared in well over 100 competitions. Yes, he's had a few injuries along the way, but he's always come back from them. That's because he's looked after his body so well. He's always been hot on his mobility and conditioning, as well as cardio exercise. Then there's Brian Shaw, who's been competing for 17 years and is still mixing it with the best in his forties. And when Mark and Brian do finally hang their belts up, they won't be hobbling about on sticks, they'll be able to function as normal human beings.

Fitness takes lots of different forms. Mo Farah is obviously extremely fit, but I look at him and think, 'He doesn't look right, he's all skin and bones.' He probably looks at me and thinks I don't look right for the opposite reason. Obviously, if I tried to do what Mo Farah does, I'd be gassed after a few hundred metres. But if Mo Farah tried to run with a 100kg sandbag, he'd be gassed after a few feet.

There'd be no point in me going out jogging, because strongman is all about being explosive over 20 or 30 metres.

But to be a successful strongman, you have to be aerobically fit. I do find myself breathing heavily for no particular reason, because of my body weight. But in training, Luke and I run with 100kg sandbags and carry shields 50 or 60 metres. That has us breathing pretty hard, but probably not as hard as some people walking along with a couple of shopping bags. I also do the '21-15-9' CrossFit workout, which involves doing each exercise for 21 reps, then 15 reps, then nine reps, as fast as possible. I was always quick off the mark, but I can now keep that pace going. That's why I almost always finish first or second in loading events, and can fill a skip with a sandbag, a tyre, a keg and an anchor in under 30 seconds.

I don't go out drinking every weekend, I don't take drugs and I don't eat junk every other night. I have some very clever people looking after my body, and I know everything's working properly, because I'm always getting checked out by doctors. Before a competition, I'll have a full body scan. And if the doctor found an irregular heartbeat, I wouldn't be allowed to compete. In fact, they'd probably tell me not to do strongman anymore. But I've never had a problem. In fact, the results of the scans show my heart has been getting stronger every year.

• • •

After finishing second at Britain's Strongest Man, I thought, 'Stuff this, I'm going to hire a proper strongman nutritionist. And if I want to be the best, I have to hire the best.' Up until then, I'd been using a nutritionist who was a bodybuilder. That didn't make much sense. So, I swapped him for an American guy called Nathan Payton, who was working with Brian Shaw, as well as lots of NFL and MMA athletes.

Nathan didn't come cheap, but I don't care much about money anyway. I'll spend money on anything that will make me better, even if I end up going skint. Besides, Nathan said that if I ever won World's Strongest Man, I'd never have to pay him again. That sounded like a pretty sweet deal.

Nathan plans everything for me – I just have to chuck the food and drink down my neck. I'll let Nathan explain the science, because I don't know what he's going on about half the time. But he basically programmes me, telling me what to eat and drink and when. And because he splits everything into proteins, carbohydrates, fats, etc., and gives me six options of each for every meal, I don't get bored.

When I'm not competing, I'll eat quite healthily. On an average day, I might eat ten fried eggs, mushrooms and four slices of bread for breakfast. For brunch, if you want to call it that, I'll have a protein shake, with a few scoops of whey, and a punnet of fruit. Lunch and dinner will be 400g of meat, whatever kind I want, two packets of rice and a pile of veg. And my pre-bed snack might be another protein shake. It's all about fuelling myself in line with my training regime, peaking at the right time each day.

People are always asking me how many calories I eat a day. I can understand that, because a lot of nutritionists are obsessed with calories. But Nathan said on day one, 'Your body can't do maths, so why would you count calories?' Once you have that in your brain, it changes everything.

The problem with sticking strictly to a certain number of calories is that your body feels different on different days. So you might end up eating a chocolate bar at night to hit your calorie intake and go to bed feeling rubbish. Or you might hit your calorie intake at dinner time and go to bed feeling famished. The point being, your body doesn't know if you've eaten a chocolate bar with 200 calories, so you have to go by how you feel. Also, if you're getting all your necessary vitamins from food, you don't need to take vitamin pills.

Basically, if I'm feeling hungry, I haven't eaten enough. If I'm feeling lethargic, I've probably overeaten. Some days, I'll text Nathan and say, 'I don't quite feel right.' And he'll reply, 'Just add an extra meal tonight and you'll feel better in the morning.' When I'm travelling, he might tell me to eat two extra 'cheat' meals, to guard against fatigue. That might be burger and chips, a pizza or a couple of rounds of sandwiches. When I hit the sack, I'll have no idea how many calories I've consumed that day. It's probably between 8–10,000, which is about four times the recommended number for an average bloke. But you have to remember that when you're as big as I am, and lifting the weights I do, those calories are constantly being burned through, like a raging wildfire.

While some people think it must be great being able to eat that much food every day, it's actually a chore. The first couple of meals are usually okay, but by dinner I'll be thinking, 'Someone order me a pizza!' You've also got to remember that I've got a wife, who occasionally wants to treat herself to a curry or a Chinese. But if it doesn't fit in with my programme,

I'll have to opt out. And if we do eat out, I'll have to order two or three starters as well as a main. Posh restaurants are a nightmare, because they serve tiny portions.

There's also a lot of trial and error when you're eating that much. I have trouble with certain foods, like brown rice and bread, which make my belly swell. Dairy also doesn't sit well with me, and after Luke and I did a burger challenge before a competition in Iceland, I spent days on the toilet. It's about finding what works and sticking to that, with variations built in.

With Nathan on board, I felt like a completely different package in 2020. He was like a food magician – every time he told me to eat something, I'd feel stronger. World's Strongest Man couldn't come soon enough.

12

PROFESSIONAL STRONGMAN

LUKE

The transition from full-time surveyor to full-time strong-man didn't go entirely to plan. That was mainly because when Covid hit at the start of 2020, I didn't have any income from competitions for the best part of a year.

In a normal year, we're never scratching around for events to compete in. There are as many as 15 to choose from, although only four or five is feasible, what with all the training involved. If you're successful, you can earn decent money from it, but probably not as much as you think. Martins Licis made about US$40,000 for winning World's Strongest Man in 2019, and that's the most prestigious competition on the calendar.

Because of the financial unpredictability of strongman, I'd been trying to get the Stoltman brand going for a couple of years before Covid. And Eddie Hall provided the blueprint. Eddie is a truly great athlete, no doubt about that. To become as insanely strong as he did and beat men who were so much bigger than him was scarcely believable. When he won World's Strongest Man in 2017, I was in tears, because I was so happy for him.

Besides winning World's Strongest Man, Eddie was also the first person to deadlift half a tonne, which was the strongman equivalent of Roger Bannister's four-minute mile, in that most people thought it couldn't be done. But Eddie realised that winning competitions and setting world records wasn't enough. To make serious money from the sport, he needed to turn himself into a brand.

Eddie understood his worth and was very good at marketing himself. He brought hype and drama to the strongman scene. When he set that deadlift world record in Leeds, he milked it for all it was worth. He understood the value of social media. He was brash and not afraid of saying what he felt, which I respected him for. He sold his own branded merchandise and turned himself into a celebrity, appearing on TV and in films. And because he transcended the world of strongman, lots of companies wanted to be associated with him.

Eddie was a true British trailblazer, showing us what was attainable by combining success in strongman with a sharp business brain. And he's a big reason why strongman is more popular than ever. But it's nowhere near as big as it could be. I look at other sports, which are multi-billion-dollar industries, and think, 'Yeah, that's pretty cool, and the athletes are very impressive, but we're lifting cars and pulling planes!' Packaged properly, strongman would be one of the most exciting sports on the planet.

The razzmatazz comes naturally, what with all the mad stuff we do. We've also got plenty of engaging characters. Problem is, strongman isn't visible enough. I don't understand why World's Strongest Man, the sport's premier event, a competition everyone in the world knows about, is broadcast months after it takes place. With media coverage comes money. And the more money involved in a sport, the sexier it seems, the more people want to do it and the more people want to watch it.

Eddie was also proof that you can be successful and make a few quid while remaining a down-to-earth person. I only really got to know him well after Mum passed away. When I went down to Newcastle to watch Tom compete, Eddie was the only guy to say he was sorry about my mum and give me a cuddle. That meant so much to me and we've been close since then. Then, a couple of years ago, Eddie invited me and Tom to his new house in Stoke, which is more like a mansion.

When we turned up at what we thought was Eddie's house, I couldn't make out the number. I phoned him and said we might be outside, and he looked through the window and replied, 'Yeah, you're at the right place.' Of course we were – it was the biggest house in the whole of Staffordshire!

Eddie had only just moved in, but he's invested serious money since. He's got a gym, a pool, a sauna, an oxygen chamber, a cryotherapy chamber, hot and cold baths and a boxing ring. Others might look at Eddie and be jealous, but I like spending time with successful people – I find it inspirational.

We trained with Eddie for a week, and he paid for everything, including our physio every day. His wife Alex even made dinner every night, which must have been like serving up a medieval banquet. Eddie was serious when it came to training but a lot of fun the rest of the time. We'd sit around talking nonsense and playing computer games, before having a wee whisky before bed. It was a very positive environment, which is key for a professional athlete.

Over in America, Brian Shaw has done a similar thing to Eddie. Brian has had his own YouTube channel for 15 years and has lots of business interests, including his own strongman competition. Meanwhile, Thor Björnsson has carved out a career as an actor and even has his own drinks company. I look at people like Eddie, Brian and Thor and think, 'They all started out the same as me and Tom, just dafties who liked lifting weights. And now they're all set for life.' It's not about the fame – that doesn't excite me. It's about creating a business in the Highlands that will secure our families' futures.

Opening the gym, which was by then the Stoltman Strength Centre, was the foundation. But with everything in lockdown, I could now concentrate on building upwards. As a strongman, you can only train a few hours a day, which leaves a lot of time to do other things if you really want to. The priority was extending and refurbishing the gym to make it more inviting for paying customers. People are often apprehensive about training with free weights rather than machines, because they associate it with roaring meatheads in spandex shorts, so we didn't want it to feel too spit and sawdust and macho.

My ambitions were getting bigger and bigger. But I'd still get people saying to me, 'Do you really think your business is going to work up here?' I had that same mentality when I started in strongman. I'd think, 'All these guys from the big cities have it easier than us. They've got the flash gyms, all the equipment, decent trainers.' Looking back, they were excuses.

If you want to be successful, you can't have excuses to fall back on. A town is just a town, and you're your own person. You have to put the effort in, wherever you're from. Look at Cheick 'Iron Biby' Sanou: he's from Burkina Faso in Africa, which wasn't a country I had heard about before I heard about him. When he started out, he had to make his own equipment and was filling a log with sand to get the right weight. Now he's one of the strongest men in the world who has set all sorts of records in the log press.

The same could be said about genetics. Genetics plays a big part in most sports, but people use it as an excuse. I'm 6ft 3in, which isn't that big by strongman standards. I could have looked at other strongmen, like the 6ft 8in Brian Shaw or the 6ft 9in Thor Björnsson, and thought, 'It's usually one of those behemoths who wins World's Strongest Man, what's the point in even trying?' Instead, I looked at guys like Mariusz Pudzianowski, who was only 6ft but won World's Strongest Man five times, or Graham Hicks, who was only 5ft 10in but a brilliant strongman. There are always going to be people with advantages in life, social and physical. But it would be a pretty desperate and gloomy world if everyone without those advantages just didn't bother trying.

When Tom and I started to sell merchandise, there were three of us stuffed into a tiny room at the back of our gym – our brother Harry taking an order down from the shelf, putting it into a bag and handing it to Tom; me printing out a label on the computer; Tom sticking the label on the bag. And when we moved into our new offices, we had no gas or electricity. But we've come on in leaps and bounds.

Harry is now fully in charge of merchandise, and our range is expanding all the time. We've brought in a couple of lads to film and edit our YouTube videos, and hired a brilliant filmmaker called Jordan Mulligan to film a feature-length documentary. We've hired a business manager and we're opening a shop in autumn 2022. We've also taken on our first sponsored athlete – Chloe Brennan, a strongwoman from Staffordshire – to promote the Stoltman brand. Then there's the Stoltman podcast, which gives us a chance to speak to some very interesting people, from the strongman world and beyond.

I'd also love to start a Stoltman Games in Invergordon, along the lines of the Brian Shaw Classic in Colorado, but with the best Highland games athletes competing as well. Highland games have been a big part of Scottish culture for centuries and it would be a real shame if they died out.

We're nowhere near where we want to be, but we're never standing still. It will take a lot of money, and we might have to beg, steal and borrow, but we'll get there. Saying that, building the business is not really about becoming rich and living high on the hog – or the fact I'd have to go back offshore if it failed, which is my worst nightmare. It's mainly about the almost childlike excitement of creating something from nothing, starting small and ending up impressive. Not much different than Granddad Stoltman getting on his bike, pedalling into the unknown and becoming the best peat cutter in Scotland.

• • •

During lockdown, Tom tried to keep the competitive juices flowing by getting involved with online streaming events, including some world-record attempts. Tom smashed one of his own world records, lifting a 286kg Atlas Stone over a four-foot bar, while I tried and failed to set a new log lift record of 230kg. I was a fraction from locking my left arm out, which I was gutted about. I already had the log press reps world record, but to beat Žydrūnas Savickas's mark would have been pretty cool.

But the odd record attempt aside, my priorities were in the wrong order. Building the business was exciting and fruitful, but it took up a lot of time and energy, physically and mentally. So, when World's Strongest Man was finally staged in November 2020, having been postponed from May, I wasn't properly prepared.

It's not as if I disgraced myself, but I wasn't able to recover from a last-placed finish in the opening event, the farmer's walk, and missed out on the finals. Not to put too fine a point on it, that hurt a lot. Having quit my 'real' job to concentrate on strongman, I'd done worse than the year before.

Because of Covid, there were no spectators in Bradenton, and we had to compete in a bubble. Luckily, Tom provided plenty of fireworks. In the finals, he won three of the five events. Only a mistake in the giant's medley, when a 125kg anvil slipped out of his hands, and a poor Hercules hold scuppered his chances of overall victory. As it was, Tom finished second, just behind Ukraine's Oleksii Novikov, who was two years younger than him at 24. He was also seven inches shorter and 40kg lighter, which meant he had to be a phenomenal technician.

During the build-up, there had been a lot of talk about who wasn't competing. Thor had retired, while defending champion Martins Licis and 2019 runner-up Mateusz Kieliszkowski were injured. But that's the nature of any athletic competition. You can only beat what's put in front of you, and Tom beat some great strongmen that year, including Canadian veteran JF Caron and Brian Shaw.

I was very impressed by the way Tom handled himself that week. He got a bit excited in the first event, and that cost him. But he brushed himself down and put in a storming performance after that. Tom didn't leave Florida with the trophy, but the writing was on the wall for the following year.

• • •

I'd had a coach for a while, an Aussie guy, Sebastian Oreb, who was, and still is, one of the best in the world. But because he lived so far away, I could only really show him video clips, which wasn't ideal. Plus, when I was working offshore, having a coach often seemed pointless, because I never knew where I'd be or when. Why have someone design a programme for me when I might be stuck on a rig for three weeks without the necessary equipment?

But after messing up at World's Strongest Man in 2020, I stepped back and took a long, hard look at my situation. Now, I didn't have any reason not to have a coach. I had the time and all the gear I needed. It's not like I was Brian Shaw, who owns every piece of strongman equipment known to man, but the more success Tom and I had, the more generous companies

Never could resist
an arm wrestle …

Kilted up with Dad
for Luke's wedding.

Messing around before Tom's wedding.

'The Nest', our first gym! The shed at the bottom of Mum and Dad's garden.

Scotland's Strongest Man 2014.

Tom and Sinead.

Where it all started for Luke, entering and winning his first competition, Highlands Strongest Man 2012.

Luke and Kushi's wedding!

Pose off at Forge
gym in Inverness.

Tom and Sinead
at FIBO 2016.

Europe's Strongest Man 2021.

Giving media interviews at World's Strongest Man.

This was a great charity event in Inverness for Marie Curie. We were invited along to give a talk about our career and about our family's story with cancer.

Always proud to represent Scotland.

Tom with his two World's Strongest Man trophies!

We couldn't do it without you, Sinead and Kushi.

became. We only had to give them a plug on social media and someone would send us something. And because it's not easy to get rid of strongman equipment, we ended up with random stuff scattered all over the place. We even had the shell of an old Ford, because we were going to set up a car walk, although we haven't got around to that yet. And we had so many spare Atlas Stones that we decided to build a sculpture out of them in Dad's garden.

A mate also let us use his warehouse, which meant we could do a lot of our more specialist strongman training in a large, dry, covered space, instead of outside. It's very basic, but it's all we need. We have bought a big blast heater for when it's really cold. But if you're cold during a workout, you're not working hard enough. Sometimes, I'd walk into the gym and the heaters would be on full blast. I'd say to the guys, 'Just put more effort in! We're paying for the electricity!' I got rid of them in the end, because it was doing my head in.

I'd seen how much Tom had improved since hooking up with Dan Hipkiss and thought he might be able to do something similar for me. One night I told Kushi I was thinking about giving Dan a call, which she thought was a great idea. Half an hour later, I got a text from Dan, saying: 'I'd really like to coach you.' I replied, 'Bloody hell, I was just talking about you! Let's do it!' Clearly it was written in the stars that we belonged together.

It was a challenge having someone doing all my program-ming, because I'd been self-sufficient for so long. But having someone in my corner, telling me exactly what I needed to do in every session, was hugely beneficial. Strongman is highly technical, so you need constant monitoring and to be told what you're doing right or wrong. And when the man in your corner is of Dan's calibre, you trust him implicitly and expect to progress at a faster rate than before.

I'm sure there are people who watch strongman on TV and think we're all just massive brutes. I thought that before I started doing it. But when you look at how specific events have changed over the years, you'll realise how much more scientific it's become. Take the log lift as an example. Watch them do it in the early 1980s and they're all ripping it off the floor, curling it onto their chests and lifting it above their heads almost in one movement. A modern strongman breaks the lift down into parts. And if one part fails, he's not going to succeed. First, he'll put the log onto his lap before using the power in his hips to hoist it onto his chest. Once he's steady, he'll complete the lift. With every event, there's a correct way of doing things now, although each athlete will have his quirks, depending on his body shape and mechanics.

To execute all these different techniques, your body needs to be properly prepared. Dan gives us all sorts of weird and wonderful exercises to maintain and improve our core stability and hip mobility. If your hip alignment is off when you're attempting a lift, your balance is also going to be off. At the same time, you must make sure your core strength is there, because if it's not, you're not going to have enough explosive power to complete the lift.

As it stands, our weekly training regime looks like this: Monday is back day, which means deadlifts and all sorts of other exercises – box jumps, face-down dumbbell rolls, single-arm pulldowns, plate-loaded rows and hollow body holds (which involves lying on our backs with our heads and feet raised, our arms above our heads and a heavy plate rested on our legs – it's a killer, but brilliant for core strength). Tuesday is pressing day – standing overhead presses, chest presses, dumbbell presses and rows, front plate raises and face pulls. Wednesday is a recovery day, consisting of mobility and physio. Thursday is legs day – and you can't skip legs day! It usually means a lot of squatting. And on Friday, we head to the warehouse, where we practise the actual events.

Some strongmen spend five or six hours in the gym, but we often do a bit less than that. That's not a problem, though, because we make our sessions very intense. And we're probably in the warehouse for four hours or so, because moving all the equipment about is a lot of faff. Then we have the weekend off, otherwise we'd probably end up killing ourselves.

I'm sure when Geoff Capes was winning his two World's Strongest Man titles in the 1980s, there were people who thought humans couldn't get any stronger. But we now look at Geoff, Bill Kazmaier and Jón Páll Sigmarsson as pioneers. They were the guys doing it for the first time, laying the ground. Still, some of those early competitions were more like a Victorian circus than sport.

In the first World's Strongest Man, in 1977, the competitors bent iron bars over their heads or round their necks, did the tug of war and took part in wheelbarrow races. In the 'refrigerator race', Italian Franco Columbu, who was Schwarzenegger's best mate, dislocated his knee, which effectively finished his body-building career.

They weren't big on safety back then, or women's rights. In 1980, they held World's Strongest Man at a Playboy club in New Jersey. There were Playboy bunnies everywhere, and I'm sure everyone had a lot of fun. But it made strongman look more like entertainment than sport, especially the 'girl lift', which required them to squat a load of giggling bunnies sat in a cage.

Most of the guys back then came from other sports and were doing strongman for a bit of fun. There were Olympic field athletes like Capes, American footballers, martial artists, wrestlers, weightlifters, powerlifters, bodybuilders, even stuntmen. Lou Ferrigno, Schwarzenegger's great rival who played the Hulk on TV, competed in the first World's Strongest Man. With a couple of exceptions, those guys turned up to strongman competitions with no practice and no strategy. It was all about lifting whatever random heavy stuff was put in front of them, and they didn't really care if they won or lost.

Some of those guys had great physiques – Ferrigno was a two-time Mr Universe, while Sigmarsson looked like a Greek god. But others just looked like big lumps down the pub, the type that could neck 15 pints without getting even slightly tipsy. Or those farmers you get who build up brute strength just by doing their jobs. Or our granddad, who got insanely strong simply because he had to.

You won't see modern strongmen bending bars over their heads or tearing telephone books in half – the crowds are watching a bona fide sport rather than a freak show. The progression of strongman records shows you how much more serious it's become. As recently as 2008, the strongman deadlift record was 410kg; Thor deadlifted 501kg in 2020, beating Eddie's world record. At World's Strongest Man in 1980, Bill Kazmaier set a new world record of 157kg in the log lift. In 2021, Iron Biby lifted 229kg. For those of you who still work in old numbers, that's an increase of about 11½ stone, or a middleweight boxer.

Modern strongmen are bigger and stronger because they're far more scientific in their approach. We train specifically for strongman – we're not just dabbling. While most of those old guys would have shovelled pretty much anything down their necks, as long as it made them feel full, our diets are far more controlled. Geoff Capes probably had the occasional massage, but we're getting proper sports physio every week, taking hot and cold baths, using cryochambers, having infrared treatment, and seeing chiropractors and acupuncturists. Tom and I have even bought a couple of hi-tech mattresses with dual climate control. Our wives can be nice and toasty on their side of the bed and we're not sweating like racehorses.

Up until recently, my hydration routine was quite ad hoc. But after my quad muscle started spasming at a recent competition, while I was attempting a deadlift, we could only surmise I hadn't hydrated enough. Now, I get my bloods checked every month and my supplements tailormade, with exact amounts of minerals and vitamins. We're also looking at getting IV drips, which are great for hydration and reducing inflammation.

Things have got so scientific I'm not sure how much stronger humans can get. Then again, I never thought anyone would deadlift 500kg, and that's now happened twice. Records are going up in tiny increments, and I'd be very surprised if someone suddenly added 10kg to the deadlift or log press world record. But the human body is capable of incredible things, and maybe if strongman organisers said, 'Next year, we're only interested in world records, nothing else will score points', we'd all train harder than we ever thought possible to make it happen. That's just how professional athletes think.

13

INTERLUDE

NATHAN PAYTON

Like a lot of people, I got into strongman almost by accident. I met a guy named Ryan Bracewell, who had just started pursuing strongman as a hobby. My dad and I had watched strongman since I was a kid. I was also involved in the supplement world and did a bit of bodybuilding. So I suggested to Ryan that maybe I could help. Ryan replied, 'Okay. Because I don't know anything about what I should be eating.'

This was the 2000s, when most strongmen were shovelling down anything and everything. Most strongmen back then didn't entertain the concept of diet influencing performance. But after I started to help Ryan, he began to get results in the gym. Sometimes he even outlifted his friend, strongman veteran Travis Ortmayer, which Travis was baffled by.

When I became partners with Ryan in a gym, he invited Travis to train with him. Travis was coming up to a big contest and asked if there was anything he could do, nutrition-wise, to peak at the right time. I gave him some pointers, and a few weeks later he won the contest.

Back then, Travis weighed about 340lb and looked like an old-school strongman. I kept telling him, 'You're fast, but if we got some of that fat off, you'd be faster.' At World's Strongest Man in 2009, Travis was down to 315lb and finished fifth. At the Arnold Classic a few months later, he was down to 275lb and finished third.

Back then, most people assumed bigger was better. Mariusz Pudzianowski, who won World's Strongest Man five times in the 2000s, looked like an Adonis, but he was an outlier. So when the other guys first saw Travis at the Arnold, they wondered what he was up to. Some of them thought he was sick. Some of them thought he was competing in the bodybuilding contest. But Travis's performance at the Arnold changed the sport. Before, most strongmen feared losing weight, because they assumed it would make them weaker. But Travis proved that losing weight could make you more effective.

After that Arnold Classic, Brian Shaw, who'd won the title, contacted me. He'd come very close to winning World's Strongest Man in 2010 and thought that if he added what I was doing with Travis, he'd win it in 2011. That's what happened. After that, Brian was telling anyone and everyone what he was doing with me, and how it had given him the extra 5 per cent he'd needed. Suddenly, every strongman understood the importance of food.

Every athlete is a unique project for me, and it's all to do with the actions and manipulation of insulin. Insulin is a hormone made in your pancreas. When you eat something, carbohydrates are broken down and changed into glucose, which is then absorbed into your bloodstream. Once the glucose is in your bloodstream, the insulin will prompt cells throughout the body to absorb the sugar and use it for energy. Insulin also helps balance your blood glucose levels. When there's too much glucose in your bloodstream, insulin tells your body to store the leftover glucose in your liver. And the stored glucose isn't released until your blood glucose levels decrease.

If an individual is naturally lean, more body fat helps. But if an individual is naturally rounder, it's the opposite. It's all to do with insulin sensitivity. In naturally lean athletes, insulin sensitivity is higher. In naturally rounder athletes, it's lower and needs to be increased.

I never count calories, it's a useless thing for elite athletes to focus on. If you want to lose weight, find out how many calories you're burning in the gym and adjust your calorie intake. But if you want your body to go outside its genetic comfort zone and do amazing things, calorie-counting is worthless.

The human body is not the same as a building. And I'm not an engineer. In my job, two plus two doesn't always equal four, because unlike a building, the human body is alive and constantly in flux. Every athlete will be different from one training session to the next. They'll also be different one competition to the next. They might have more muscle or less. They might have been injured. Their insulin sensitivity might be different because of a change in temperature, or other environmental influences, including stress.

Not only that, but every athlete responds differently to specific events. Tom can lift stones in his sleep, but a circus dumbbell is an all-out assault on his body. The stress of that event will cause his cortisol levels to go through the roof, and cortisol levels affect insulin sensitivity. Because of all this, I'm constantly adjusting food intake, fine-tuning athletes almost to the gram.

When an athlete arrives at a competition, I feed him to see how high his glucose levels will go. I call that peak 'the sweet spot', when I know his tank is full. And during the competition, it's all about trying to keep him at that sweet spot. Here's an example. At the Arnold Classic in 2020, one of the events was the wheel of pain, which involved pushing a huge wheel as far as possible. Beforehand, Martins Licis, the former world champion and another of my athletes, kept telling me he was full. But he wasn't at his sweet spot. And I knew that whenever Martins did an event involving leg churn, his leg muscles sucked a huge amount of glucose out of his bloodstream.

So, I kept shovelling food into him, right up until he walked out for the wheel of pain. Sure enough, he put in an incredible performance. While he was on his back, with an oxygen mask over his face, I ran over and pricked his finger, to check his glucose levels. In that minute and a half, his glucose levels had halved, so anything less than his sweet spot would have been a problem, greatly reducing performance.

When I first started working with Tom, he looked more like a bodybuilder than a strongman. Tom was eating a lot of lean meat and rice, which is a diet to look a certain way. And my focus isn't aesthetics, it's performance. So, I added more fat components, while still keeping him healthy. I also got him to focus on when to eat certain things. Timing is everything.

I'm responsible for everything Tom and Luke put in their mouths, 365 days a year. But I don't want to make them neurotic. To that end, I provide a blueprint. I'll tell them they need to eat X amount of grams of proteins or Y amount of grams of carbohydrates at a certain time, but if they're over a little bit, they're going to be okay. The body ebbs and flows throughout the day and its reaction to certain foods can dull if you eat too much of them. Plus, it's important they enjoy what I'm telling them to eat.

It's my job to fit food into an athlete's life, not disrupt and create a bunch of rules that they have to follow. I give different choices depending on whether or not they've got time to cook. I give choices for if they're travelling. I give choices for if they're focusing on recovery or if they're fuelling up for a competition. I give choices during a competition, when they need to be eating as much as possible. Of course, there is a scientific reason I tell them to eat burgers and pizzas. But I do sometimes say, 'Here's your rubbish to eat.'

There are foods that are very important to me, but if a client doesn't like something or it doesn't agree with them, I won't put it on the list. It's my job to be creative and find a similar item that can take its place. I've had clients who flat out refused to eat fruit or vegetables, so I had to make up for that with supplementation.

The one thing I won't move on is milk, because some people's bodies are very sensitive to it. When an athlete hires me, they want to see improvements fast, and I don't have time to figure out if they're one of the guys who can function well on milk or one of the guys who can't. An ice cream or a milkshake as part of a cheat meal probably isn't going to be a problem. But I'd never recommend milk as a regular part of an athlete's diet.

I'm not one of those people who thinks protein drinks are the devil. They can be useful for strength athletes, because they give your digestive system a break. Eating six or seven meals a day is very stressful. And the more food you have in your body, the more blood flow is being diverted from working muscles to the intestines and the digestive system.

Saying that, I prefer my clients to get most of their nutrition from actual food. Some protein shakes market their product as being rapidly absorbing. But the body isn't designed to be bombarded – it's designed for nutrients to be absorbed in a controlled manner. The same goes for lots of vitamins and minerals. Take vitamin D, for example. The body wants to consume it how it's found in nature, which is in a fat environment, which helps slow and maximise absorption.

My athletes have won seven World's Strongest Man titles since 2011. I've also worked with actors, MMA athletes, bikini models, powerlifters, baseball players and American footballers. Each person is a different puzzle to solve, and there are still things I haven't figured out. I'm always wondering why things didn't go as expected. Or if they did go as expected, I wonder how I can make them even better. If one of my guys has a bad session, I can't just let it go. It eats away at me – I have to make sense of it. Some of it is pride in my programme's design, some of it is basic curiosity. And if I can get better at my job, the guys I work with will get better, which is ultimately what it's all about.

It's a lot of hard work, but it's incredibly rewarding. And while some people might think I'm a Dr Frankenstein figure, trying to create the perfect specimen, I prefer to think of myself as a proud parent, trying to create as many opportunities as possible for their child to succeed. When one of my guys does great, I cry, because I know they've dramatically changed their lives. They've opened the door to more money, more public exposure and they've added to their legacy. When one of my guys does poorly, I cry as well, because those doors remain closed, despite how much hard work they've put in and all the sacrifices they've made. Win or lose, it's very emotionally draining.

As with Tom winning World's Strongest Man the first time, when Luke won Europe's Strongest Man, I watched him standing proudly on the podium. I could see all his doubts had been erased. Now that he'd achieved something he previously didn't think was possible, he knew he was capable of reaching the next level, and the next level after that.

I often compare strongmen to Formula 1 cars. They all look kind of the same, but there are so many subtle differences. Plus, in both strongman and F1, there are so many variables. In a Grand Prix, will your car brush another car? Will a brake pad fly off? Will a piston blow out? In strongman, something might slip out of your hand in the loading medley, or you might stumble during the Atlas Stones. Even the best-laid plans can turn out a little bit wild.

The Stoltmans can win anything they want to win. It's just a case of making sure they're always in good enough condition, just like a well-engineered F1 car, then sending them out to compete and seeing what happens.

14

VISUALISING SUCCESS

TOM

C ovid was tough on me at times, for the same reasons as everyone else. But because Luke and I had our own gym, and we were professional athletes, we could at least carry on training as normal, even if there was nothing in the diary to train for. I still had routine, which was key.

Looking back, I was lucky. Covid was in some ways, for me at least, a blessing in disguise. For months, my life consisted of eating, sleeping, going to the gym and hanging out with Sinead. And while it was weird having no-one else in the gym apart from Luke, it focused the mind. Those first few months of Covid, I shifted into a higher gear. I didn't know when World's Strongest Man would take place, but I knew that when it did, I'd be better prepared than I'd ever been.

Sometime over the summer of 2020, we finally got word that World's Strongest Man would take place that November. And 12 weeks out, I got down to intensive training. Boarding the plane to Florida, I felt in perfect nick. Gone were most of the negative thoughts – I thought I could lift pretty much anything.

I'm often asked what I think about before a lift. Well, in the early days there would often be a lot of negativity. But now things were different. I even had different mindsets for different lifts. Before I broke the stones world record during the Covid lockdown, I thought, 'If I don't lift this, Sinead is going to die.' It sometimes helps to go to those dark places. But having dark thoughts can sap your energy, which isn't ideal when you're in an actual competition. So, most of the time, I visualise a lift before I attempt it. And 99 per cent of the time, I nail it. I call it visualising success, and it works in any walk of life. If you visualise achieving a goal, you'll also get an idea of what achieving that goal feels like, which will make you want to go out and do it for real.

I visualise almost everything in my life. Before I go on a journey, I'll visualise the route. Before I head off to a competition, I'll visualise exactly what I need to do to win it. For weeks, that visualisation will be going round my head. Sometimes I'll think, 'Am I taking this visualisation stuff too far?' But it works. As soon as that 286kg Atlas Stone arrived in our gym during lockdown, I started visualising lifting it over the bar. I was doing that for days. And when the time came to attempt the world record, I knew exactly what to do, because I'd already done it hundreds of times in my head.

Luke and I had to wear masks on the plane to America, which I struggled with. And once we arrived in Florida, we were pretty much locked in our hotel rooms. I got why we had to do it, but not having any freedom was difficult to deal with. At least restaurants were still delivering food, because pretty much the only thing we could do was eat. Not that we had anyone else to eat with, because Sinead and Kushi had to stay at home.

You might be surprised to hear what Nathan tells us to eat in the lead-up to a competition – a load of processed muck containing lots of dirty calories! First, I'll have a burger and chips before the gym, and maybe three or four doughnuts throughout the day. During the week of a competition, when we've stopped training, it's a case of getting as much dirty food down our necks as possible, stuff that contains a lot of fast-acting sugars and gives us as much energy as possible. It sounds incredibly unhealthy, and consuming 10–12,000 calories a day would be for most people. But strongmen aren't most people, and I can feel myself getting more powerful as the week goes on.

World's Strongest Man is very specific, because it's spread over a week, and we only do two or three events a day. In the morning, I'd have a stack of eight pancakes for breakfast, plus bacon and eggs and some fruit. Three hours later, I'd have a burger, before doing my first event. Then I'd have another burger before doing my second event. In the evening, I'd have a big bowl of pasta, with lots of meat, and a whole cheesecake. Then I might eat a whole pizza as a pre-bedtime snack. But it was all stuff Nathan had told me to eat, and I trusted him. The organisers pay for the athletes' food in the hotel, but they don't serve what we need, so we have to order it in. That means it's bloody expensive. But while most of my competitors are eating whatever's on the hotel buffet for free, which might not be right for them, I'm eating properly.

I finished second behind Oleksii Novikov in my group, before beating Canada's Maxime Boudreault to reach the finals. Looking at the events in the finals, the Hercules hold appeared to be my only weak point. I thought if I scored well in every other event, I had a chance of winning.

I did everything right beforehand, which basically meant doing hardly anything, eating right and getting my head in the right place. Unfortunately, in the first event of the finals – the giant's medley – I made a hash of it. The very first thing I had to lift was a 125kg anvil (that's about 20 stone) and I got off to a flyer, leaving JF Caron for dust. But a few metres from the line, it slipped out of my hands. I managed to scoop the anvil up again, and even managed to overhaul JF with the yoke, but my time was only good enough for fifth.

A couple of years earlier, my head would have gone and my competition would have been over. I'd have thought, 'What's the point? There's no way I can win it now. I probably won't even finish in the top three.' As it was, Luke took me aside and said, 'Tom, you still came fifth, despite the mistake. Get it out of your system and let's smash the next event.'

I happily admit, having Luke with me was almost cheating. Everyone else was in their own little bubble, without their friends, family and coaches, but I had my big brother to support me. Throughout that competition, all I could hear was his deep, rumbling voice, drowning out everyone else's. And now he'd come up with the perfect pep talk. After that chat with Luke, I was able to put a positive spin on things. I thought, 'I dropped the anvil but still beat five of my rivals. That's a massive achievement, so I'm obviously in pretty good form.'

I came fifth in the partial deadlift (in which the bar starts 18 inches off the floor), which meant I was miles behind leader

Novikov, who set a mad new world record of 537.5kg (that's about 85 stone, or about three of me). I finished ninth in the Hercules hold but won the other three events – the keg toss, the log ladder and the Atlas Stones – to finish second overall, just a few points behind Novikov.

Far from being down, my performance in Bradenton sparked a fire in my belly. Back in 2018, I'd given myself the target of winning World's Strongest Man in three years. Since then, I'd finished fifth and second. Some people compete in World's Strongest Man for ten years and never make a final, but I'd become the first Scotsman and the first person with autism to finish on the podium in only my third appearance.

Plus, I *knew* I was the strongest man on the planet. I'd won three of the six events, and I might have won the giant's medley if not for a silly mistake. I'd go back to Scotland, sit down with my team and work out how to add another one or two per cent. Then I'd be ready to demolish everyone.

• • •

Britain's Strongest Man was postponed from January 2021, so my first event of the year was a World's Ultimate Strongman competition in Bahrain in March. It had a mystery event, which turned out to be a flag hoist. I finished ninth out of 15 in that event, before failing to record a lift in the dumbbell press. That meant I finished fifth overall, behind Luke in fourth. I hadn't expected that after my showing in Florida. I don't think anybody had.

Jordan filmed the competition for the documentary that Luke mentioned, and when we watched the rushes, my body language was off. I liked routine, and the mystery event had thrown me out of kilter. I might have been the strongest man in the world physically, but not mentally. I was convinced I had the best coach and nutritionist, but maybe I needed someone to look at my mind.

When we got back from Bahrain, Luke recommended a psychologist he'd met in Newcastle. Amy Izycky wasn't strictly a sports psychologist, but she had worked with some high-level athletes. Luke thought she might be able to help me, but I was dead against it at first. Doing anything new makes me anxious, and I was worried she'd mess up my routine ahead of World's Strongest Man, which was only a few months away. But after a week or so, I thought, 'Stuff it, let's give it a go. I'll soon know if it doesn't agree with me.'

I was a bag of nerves before meeting Amy for the first time. But as soon as she started talking, I knew she was special. When you're autistic, someone can say something to you, and it will go in one ear and out the other. Sometimes even Luke will say something, and I'll think, 'You don't have autism, so you don't know what you're talking about.' But because Amy knew all about autism, she was able to speak to me on my level, which I'd never experienced from a professional before. And she took my mind to places it had never been.

It was confusing at first, because Amy and my coach Dan were communicating with me in different ways. But after Amy spoke to Dan, we were soon all singing from the same hymn sheet. Amy realised I was a concrete thinker and needed simple trigger words, rather than complicated instructions.

For example, someone telling me to lift a weight ten times in a minute will confuse me. But if I walk into the gym and someone says, 'Be aggressive', my mind will clear, and I'll know exactly what to do.

It took Dan a while to get used to Amy's new methods, and I'd sometimes have to remind him he was using too many words. But we eventually reached the stage where we'd boiled it down to one or two trigger words for each event. Dan says he got to know me so well, he felt like he was living inside my brain.

Amy was big on 'centring', which is all about increasing focus, relieving stress and being in the perfect mental state for training and competitions. With me, it's simple things, like going for a walk every day. I never thought just going for a walk could make such a difference, but it did. I also started shaking my legs a lot. That might come across as a nervous thing, but it's actually another centring technique. Luke's different, he likes to chill out before competitions, lie on his bed watching stuff on his tablet for hours on end. But because I've got more nervous energy, I need to release it in some way. So, I'll go for a 15-minute wander on my own, which calms me down.

It was mindboggling what Amy could do – she seemed to know my mind better than I did. And she was as effective through a computer screen as she was in person. For the first time in my life, I felt in complete control of my mind.

If I had a bad day's training and was feeling a bit down, I'd get on a call with Amy and she'd weave her magic. By the end of the call, I'd be positive and ready to hit the gym again. But Amy didn't just talk to me about training and competitions.

If I'd been doing stuff with sponsors or had too many meetings, Amy would recognise that immediately. She'd say to me, 'Right, Tom, I can tell you've had a stressful week. Let's talk about that.' And we'd spend the next hour discussing how to manage my time better.

When I talk to Amy, it's like she's drawing all the stress out of me. And she'll find ways to prevent me getting stressed again. That's why if I miss a week with her, for whatever reason, my mind goes a bit haywire.

In the months leading up to World's Strongest Man in 2021, my main priority was improving my weaker events. With the Hercules hold, I'd get to 20 seconds, tell myself it was hurting and let go. So, I discussed it with Amy, Amy spoke to Dan and he gave me three wee words to focus on: 'Be aggressive', and 'Squeeze'. It sounds incredibly simple, but it worked. Within a couple of months, I was doing the Hercules hold for over a minute.

Another of my weakest events was the dumbbell press. I'd have seven or eight bits of information rattling around my head while I was putting my straps on. Stuff like, 'Make sure you don't lift it to there, because you won't be able to finish the press.' I was like a golfer, obsessing about his grip, ball position and swing before hitting the ball. Chances are, if he just walks up to the ball and whacks it, with a blank mind, he'll get a better result. Amy watched videos of me competing and said, 'Right, I can see you're overthinking it. You're pacing back and forth, fiddling with your straps. We need you walking straight up to the dumbbell and lifting it – bang! – like you do in the

Atlas Stones.' So I started saying, 'You're the world's strongest man. Be aggressive', and soon I was hitting dumbbell reps I'd never hit before.

I suppose you could say concrete thinking created tunnel vision. Luke could talk to me while I was preparing for a lift, and it wouldn't bother me at all. I'd be aware of a stone or a log and nothing else. But if I did the same to Luke, I'd break his concentration and he wouldn't be able to lift. Luke also couldn't have anyone in his eyeline while he was lifting in the gym, while I'd have Sinead's mates dancing in front of me and it wouldn't bother me at all.

I'd also learned it was impossible to peak for every competition, that my focus had to be on the big ones – namely World's and Britain's Strongest Man. I could understand why guys competed regularly on the Giants Live tour, because they wanted to earn money. But when you compete as often as that, you're far more likely to burn out or get a career-wrecking injury.

Look at Mateusz Kieliszkowski, who was runner-up at World's Strongest Man in 2018 and 2019. Most people assumed he was a future world champion, but he had a packed schedule in 2019, missed World's Strongest Man in 2020 with a tricep injury and has hardly been seen since.

Being at home with your feet up while your rivals are competing isn't laziness, it's being smart. And, anyway, those other competitions don't matter so much in the grand scheme of things. Kieliszkowski won six of the 12 competitions he entered in 2019, but he didn't win World's Strongest Man, so his profile outside the strongman world isn't huge. World's

Strongest Man is the only competition that gets you into the mainstream media and leads to opportunities outside the world of strongman. Besides, I didn't want strongman to rule my life. If Rangers were playing Celtic at Ibrox, I wanted to be watching that instead of competing in some minor competition.

A few weeks out from World's Strongest Man, Amy, Dan and I had things perfect. I'd never felt stronger physically and mentally. All over my house was written, 'Tom Stoltman – World's Strongest Man 2021.' Every day, Dan texted me the same. Those words became ingrained on my eyeballs, so I could visualise them wherever I went.

Once again, Sinead couldn't come with me to America, because of Covid. So, I decided to spend extended periods away from her to replicate the loneliness I'd feel before and during the competition. But we did sit down together a few times and outline exactly how I was going to win it. In those discussions, it always came down to me and Brian Shaw in the final event, the Atlas Stones. And I'd always win it by one or two points.

15

BUILDING A STRONGMAN

LUKE

W e've got some great athletes coming to our gym, and if they're actually competing in anything, whether it's running, CrossFit or bodybuilding, I'll tell them they can train for free. We only charge £25 a month membership, but that's a lot of money for some people just starting out in a sport.

Some of the youngsters are obsessed with the gym. They spend four or five hours a day in there, just like me when I started getting into lifting things. It's great to see that passion and drive up close – makes me feel like I'm giving something back.

Not every guy or girl who uses our gym will become a professional athlete, but they're all learning the same lessons: with discipline and hard work you can improve yourself. With self-improvement comes self-confidence. And you can use that confidence to prosper at whatever it is you love. That's why I'd love to franchise Stoltman gyms all over the UK, not just for financial reasons, but because I know how beneficial they'd be to communities.

Maybe one or two youngsters might look at Tom and me and think, 'Why can't I do what they've done?' And I'd love to find a rough diamond in our gym. We'd sponsor them as long as they remained dedicated, and do everything we could to get them on the strongman or strongwoman circuit. One lad called Luke is showing promise – he's bench-pressing 115kg and he's only 15. But another of our protégés is even closer to home.

Our brother Harry trained with Tom when he was starting out, but while he enjoyed the craic of the gym, he didn't have the same passion. When Harry left school, he started working offshore. Then he got married and had a baby. That's a lot of responsibility. And he felt content, so he didn't feel the need to chase anything else. But when his marriage collapsed a couple of years ago, everything changed.

I won't go into the details, but the fallout from Harry's marriage breakdown was brutal, with so many people affected. And because Mum wasn't around, I felt a responsibility to look after him. Harry had two choices: either feel sorry for himself and mope around for months or take the view that whatever doesn't kill you can make you stronger. Thankfully, he chose the latter. He quit his job offshore, joined the family business at the end of 2020 and threw himself into strongman training. Now, he's in as good a place as he's ever been. And he's got a couple of trainers who know a thing or two about lifting weights.

We've been chronicling Harry's journey in a series of YouTube videos, titled 'Building a Strongman'. Tom and I don't wear lab coats, but we do feel like a couple of mad professors from a Marvel comic, trying to create the perfect human specimen.

Harry had all the raw materials – he's 6ft 5in and was over 17 stone before he started serious strongman training in December 2021. But having all those advantages – the genes, an experienced coaching team, all the equipment – doesn't mean he's going to be successful in the sport. He has to put the work in, like anyone else. Thankfully, he is doing it.

Within a few months, Harry was almost 20 stone. He still doesn't have a power belly, but that will come. He's not ready for competitions yet, but there's no hurry and we'll know when he's ready. In the meantime, he's eating like a machine, including giant bowls of pasta when he's not even hungry. And he's lifting heavier and heavier weights.

When the time comes for him to start competing, he won't feel too intimidated, because he's known all the other guys for years. Maybe he'll feel a bit of pressure, because of his brothers' success. But he's very level-headed, and I genuinely believe he'll be a very good strongman one day. Just imagine it: in a few years' time, there could be three Stoltmans competing in World's Strongest Man. What a story that would be. But for that to happen, I needed to make a few changes.

After I'd hooked Tom up with Amy, she asked if I could do with some help too. I told her I was fine. Then I thought, 'She's doing good things with Tom, I might as well give it a crack.' And she soon made me realise I was actually a bit messed up.

Because Amy is a clinical psychologist, she was more about what and why I thought about stuff, and why I acted how I did. Before I started speaking to her, I thought I was just some idiot from Invergordon. I thought I'd got lucky, been in the right place at the right time. Deep inside, I knew I'd done pretty well for myself. But it was that negative mindset, where your glass is always half-empty, rather than half-full.

I also think my granddad's mindset had been passed down to me. For him, life was mainly about survival, grafting as hard as possible to provide for his family. He didn't think anything he'd done was special – he just thought that was living. So when I looked at what I'd done, it didn't seem right to believe it amounted to much.

In one of the first exercises Amy did with me, she asked why I thought I was an idiot. I said I played up in competitions sometimes, said silly things, once got myself a spray tan that turned me orange, so I looked like a giant Oompa Loompa. When I was finished, Amy said, 'Right. Now tell me why you're *not* an idiot.' I started listing all the things I'd achieved. I had a great family, a great wife. I'd built a house, opened a gym, started a business. I'd become a full-time athlete and was one of strongest men in the world.

When I'd finished, Amy said, 'So why do you keep calling yourself an idiot?' I told her I didn't want to come across as cocky or arrogant. And she replied, 'You're not being cocky or arrogant if you're just stating facts. Be happy with what you've achieved. Be proud of yourself. Be okay with saying you're not an idiot.' I thought, 'Yeah, that makes a lot of sense.' It didn't mean strolling around Invergordon telling everyone how great I was. It was about thinking, 'You've worked hard, you are successful, and that's a good thing.'

My mind works differently to Tom's, so Amy takes a different approach with me. While Tom's thinking is very concrete, in that once he understands something, he can just get on with it, I'm more up and down emotionally. And I had lots going on apart from my training, which was frying my brain.

In August 2021, we moved into new premises just off Invergordon High Street. Before then, Tom, Harry and I had been squeezed into a tiny office in the gym. I'd be sat at the desk, and Tom and Harry would be on the couch, and we could barely move. The new place had loads of space, including a separate office for the multimedia lads and a couple of rooms to store merchandise. But some days I'd arrive at the office at 7am and be there until one or two o'clock the following morning. When I told Amy this, she said, 'Now that *is* you being an idiot. You have to have boundaries and know what's important to you.'

I told Amy I thrived when I spent time with Kushi. That if Kushi wasn't supportive, we wouldn't be together. That for Kushi to be supportive, she had to be happy. And that when she was happy, I was happy. So, Amy advised me to make sure I was home by seven o'clock at the latest. Anything not vitally important could wait until tomorrow. She advised me to have dinner with Kushi, watch a film with her, go for a walk with the dogs together. She said we should spend quality time together after a major competition. It sounded like stupid little things, but those little things aren't stupid at all. Added together, they matter.

Without Kushi, I'd probably be in a lonely place. In fact, I'm not sure I'd be where I am in life. I know Kushi will always be proud of me, whatever happens. And I know she'll back me in anything I decide to do, whether it's strongman, opening a new gym or trying to forge a career as a voiceover artist (coming to you in an ad break soon, Luke Stoltman extolling the virtues of porridge oats – you never know …). I hope Kushi realises I'd do the same for her – that whatever she wants to do, however bonkers, I'll do everything I can to support her.

Mine and Kushi's life together isn't perfect. Sometimes we have bad days, and our marriage went through a rocky patch when my mum died, because I found it difficult to accept that Kushi's parents were still alive and well, when in my family, Mum was gone and the rest of us were grieving. But it would be weird if we didn't have bad days, unhealthy even. Kushi brings out every feeling in me, mostly positive, but sometimes negative. And that's when you know you're really in love: when everything feels so real.

I stopped spending so much time in the office. I started trusting that everyone else involved in the business was doing a good job. My role was to think about the bigger stuff – how to grow the business, where we needed to be in four or five years' time. And to start training like a bona fide professional strongman.

When Jordan started filming the documentary, I could never say I wanted to win World's Strongest Man. When he asked who I'd choose between me and Tom winning it, I said Tom. That's what I truly believed, because I thought it would probably make more difference if Tom won it, give a big boost to the autistic community or anyone with additional needs. But after a few months working with Amy, I started to think, 'You know what? You've had your own issues and you've been on your own inspirational journey. You've struggled with your mental health, and you've struggled with self-doubt.'

It also struck me that Tom didn't have any qualms about saying he wanted to win World's Strongest Man. And he didn't just want to win it for other people anymore, like Mum or Sinead. He wanted to win it for himself. Yes, there was a great energy between us, and we thrived off each other in training. But when it came to competing, Tom was an island, and rightly so.

So, my mindset flipped. I realised it was okay to say I wanted to win World's Strongest Man. And I didn't just want to win that title, I *needed* to win it. Not just that, but I was so full of confidence, I really thought I would win it one day.

I wish I'd started working with Amy five years earlier. Every time I speak to her, it's like there are fireworks going off in my head. With Amy on board, Team Stoltman feels bulletproof. As far as I am concerned, we have the best coach, psychologist and nutritionist in the world.

Nathan's attention to detail is incredible, as you would expect from a guy whose clients have won seven of the last 14 World's Strongest Man titles. He has a whole ton of qualifications, and I don't understand some of the big, fancy words he uses. But when you've got a guy like that telling you what to eat, you don't spend any time second guessing.

My dietary requirements are similar to Tom's, but we don't eat exactly the same thing, simply because he's a lot bigger than me. When Tom eats ten eggs for breakfast, I'll eat eight. When he eats 340 grams of meat, I'll eat 300 grams. People assume athletes eat dozens of chickens a week, but I find it difficult eating poultry day in, day out. However, I do eat a lot of red meat, like steak mince. Red meat is more calorie-dense than chicken anyway, and it boosts testosterone levels, which is very important for a strongman.

Hats off to bodybuilders, whose diets are incredibly clean and involve regimented food-prepping, but because strongmen consume so much more food, it has to be enjoyable. I'm a big fan of Rice Krispies, so will often have a big bowl of them after a workout. Like any true Scotsman, porridge is a staple for me, and I eat more of it than Tom. Nathan frowns upon white sauces with meat, but we can have tomato-based sauces.

When we're at a competition, Nathan will give us constant updates. For example, he'll text to remind us to eat an energy-boosting Rice Krispie bar 20 minutes before an event. Even when we're not competing, he'll constantly be asking how we feel. Only the other day, I texted him after training to tell him I felt 'like a beast'. He loved that, because he'd just tweaked my diet slightly.

As long as Tom and I are improving, we're happy. But I am a lot more inquisitive than Tom. Tom doesn't like to think about anything other than lifting things. He gets told what to do and does it, and not much else. I like to look deeper, searching for anything that might make me a slightly better athlete. As far as I'm concerned, that's me doing my job properly as a professional.

Amy made me far more aware of my feelings – how to control them, how to respond to them. Besides the obvious things that made me happy – spending time with Kushi, hanging out with the lads, training with Tom – I was suddenly more in tune with the smaller, simpler things in life. So many people are chasing a Hollywood version of happiness – five-star hotels, Michelin-starred restaurants, designer threads, flash cars, big watches, massive houses – and get sad or upset if they don't have Wi-Fi and can't look at social media. But I took a step back and realised that happiness can be eating a simple meal, having a hot shower, drinking an ice-cold glass of water, putting on a fresh pair of socks, getting cosy under a blanket. The kinds of things I used to take for granted but so many people in the world can't do.

I earn considerably more now than I ever did offshore, and I was doing pretty well before I quit. But, for the most part, I don't do extravagances. Gone are the days when I spent loads of money on expensive clothes and watches. I'm just as happy in a cheap pair of trainers and one of our own sweatshirts. Besides, being flash doesn't go down very well in Invergordon.

I get through quite a few sofas, because of my size, and we'll pay for upgrades when we fly to competitions, because we can't be hunched up for hours. Food isn't cheap. At World's Strongest Man in Sacramento, Tom and I spent $3,000 on food, and our food expenses for a year are astronomical. But that's what we have to do to be successful.

I've been to Abu Dhabi and Dubai, with the fancy shops and restaurants, and while you can have fun there, it's very artificial. All those tall, glass buildings aren't a patch on the view across the Cromarty Firth.

Tom has treated himself to a personalised number plate, and he buys a bottle of nice aftershave whenever he wins a competition. He has one spray and never wears it again. Oh, he also once bought himself a Gucci wallet. Two days later, it fell out of his pocket on Alness High Street and a car ran over it. But apart from that, he's pretty low-key.

For Christmas 2021, we bought Dad a new pickup truck, a top of the range Toyota Hilux, to say thanks for everything he's done. It was great to be able to do that, although I'm worried we set the bar way too high. He's going to be very disappointed when he gets a pair of slippers next year.

One of my favourite things is taking a dip in a loch or the sea. Sometimes, I'll go out in the North Sea in the height of winter, when it's pitch dark and the waves are almost taking my head off. And when Loch Morlich freezes over, we find a hole in the ice and jump in. Most people do that sort of stuff in a wetsuit, but we do it in just our Speedos. And while we usually do it attached to a rope, I once made the mistake of doing it without one. The current started taking me away under the ice, I couldn't see the hole and I started panicking. I genuinely thought I was going to die. Not surprisingly, YouTube told us to take that video down.

When I started working offshore, I was told a human could only last three minutes in the North Sea before getting hypothermia and dying. But I love putting my body in extreme situations and defying expectations. And while we started taking those dips as a bit of fun, we soon realised it made us feel good, which is all that really matters. I'd be buzzing afterwards, deliriously happy. It also helped with my sleep. Because of my size, I get something called sleep apnoea, which is when your oxygen cuts off and you stop breathing. You automatically wake up, but it does affect the quality of your sleep. Tom and I have special machines to combat it, but cold water also seems to do the trick.

We had a mate who was struggling a bit mentally, and he found taking dips in the sea really helped him. Starting just after Christmas, he did it every day for six weeks. One day, it was -16°C. I don't know the science behind it, but he highly recommends it. Mind you, it's not for everyone. If Tom wasn't a strongman, he'd go nowhere near the sea. As he sometimes says, he can think of lots of better things to be doing on a Friday night.

Some of my fondest memories are of being on the beach after a swim, making a fire with Kushi or some friends, getting warm and chatting about nothing in particular. Sod five-star hotels, it's not possible to be happier than me on that beach.

I also started doing meditation and breathing exercises. I visited a little old lady who was a shamanic teacher. She lived in the middle of nowhere but was lovely, very in tune with nature. She did drumming and I reacted really well to the vibrations. She also explained about journeying to lower and upper worlds. I didn't understand a lot of what she was talking about, but I think anything that makes you feel good is worth doing. Unsurprisingly, Tom didn't share my enthusiasm for shamanism. He's cool with hot and cold baths, and tolerates the odd dip in the sea, but anything too hippy is his worst nightmare. He'd have seen that little old lady, thought she was a witch and legged it.

In taking more time for things that made me feel good, I also got to spend more time with Dad. He'd take the dogs for a walk, give me a call and ask if I fancied some breakfast. We'd chat about life offshore, comparing horror stories. Like the time I was out in Angola, measuring up some pipework on a big ship. We were down in the bowels, knee deep in oil and sludge, when I loosened a bolt. Then we heard a hiss. Chris, the guy I was working with, shouted, 'It's leaking! Tighten it up and let's get out of here!' That was a narrow escape, we could have been killed.

When we got back on deck, the Angolan workers, who did most of the proper hard graft and were usually the dirty ones, complained about us because we were covered in sludge and slime and stank to high heaven. We had to take off our boiler suits and have a cup of tea in our pants.

While I stayed offshore for far too long, I did have plenty of fun along the way. Working offshore is a bit like being in the military, in that it's gangs of lads living and working in each other's pockets for months on end, often very far from home. You form strong bonds when you're thrown together like that, and I'm still good friends with a lot of my old colleagues.

But reminiscing with Dad didn't leave me hankering to go back on the rigs – it made me even more appreciative of my current situation. Even now, I'll wake up at 4am in a cold sweat, thinking I'm out on a rig in Papua New Guinea or some other far-flung place. When I realise I'm actually in Invergordon, and have another couple of hours in bed, the relief is immense. Or

I'll be feeling a bit stressed and think, 'Jesus, I've got some filming to do, that's all. It's not a bad way to spend a day – certainly better than almost dying in the bowels of a ship in Angola, while up to your knees in oil and sludge.'

16

INTERLUDE

DR AMY IZYCKY

trained as a clinical psychologist but was also a high-performance rower and have been working with sportspeople since early in my career. In reductionist terms, the job of a sports psychologist is to enhance the performance of individuals with quite solid baselines, people who are mentally managing. But a clinical psychologist works with individuals who are functioning below a stable baseline, people who are mentally struggling.

Some sports psychologists have done further training in therapeutic models and might be able to offer a piece of short-term intervention. But often, a sportsperson will be seeing a sports psychologist for a diagnosable mental health condition when perhaps they should be seeing a clinical psychologist.

Sportspeople often assume a clinical psychologist won't be able to understand them, because not all have a high-performance sports background. Or maybe they're in an environment that has outdated attitudes, with managers and coaches who see mental health difficulties as weaknesses. But thankfully, attitudes are changing.

Professional sportspeople possess certain traits that allow them to operate in a very demanding environment. But those same traits can cause problems in everyday life. As such, it's an area that can't be neglected anymore, in the same way concussion and chronic traumatic encephalopathy (CTE) in contact sports can no longer be neglected.

A few years ago, I approached Luke to take part in a book I was writing, specifically a chapter on obsessionality. Luke was happy to explore his vulnerabilities, because he understood that having insight into those vulnerabilities might translate into improved performance. He even volunteered to appear on the front cover.

In March 2021, Luke contacted me and said he wanted to chat about Tom. They'd just competed in Bahrain, and Luke had beaten Tom. Luke noticed that Tom had struggled mentally, partly because of a mystery event the organisers had included. For someone with autism, who needs familiarity and predictability, having something sprung on you like that can put you at a big disadvantage.

World's Strongest Man was in a few months' time, and Luke asked if there was anything I could do to help Tom. I told Luke I was happy to meet and asked if he'd be okay working with me indirectly, in support of Tom. That's something I often do when I'm working with individuals with neurodiverse profiles. Luke being the dutiful big brother, of course he said yes.

My first meeting with Tom was virtual, but I could tell he was nervous. Thankfully, it soon became clear we were a really good fit. I trained in neuropsychology, which is to do with brain function, anatomy and injury. And occupationally, I had experience of learning disabilities and developmental delays. I also think it helped that I was quite young to be trained in my area. I wasn't the stereotypical psychoanalyst that many have come to expect, namely an old guy with a beard who somewhat resembles Freud himself!

Psychoanalysis is scary for a lot of people. There is a tradition of psychoanalysts as stony-faced blank slates, who tell their patients nothing about themselves because they need their patients to project onto them. I understand that tradition, and boundaries are important to me. But I don't think internalising stony-faced distance is the best way for a patient to move forwards. You need to be human so that patients can connect.

Psychoanalysis also involves delving into childhoods, and the idea that parents might be blamed for how a patient's character has developed can frighten people. But it's not about apportioning blame, it's simply about understanding that our formative years shape us and influence the decisions we make. And you don't require a diagnosable mental health condition to find psychoanalysis helpful. It's more about being curious, wanting to understand how your mind works. For example, am I okay that my unconscious is driving me in this direction when consciously I want something different?

In psychology, we characterise thinking as either concrete or abstract. Abstract thinking includes anything that hasn't happened yet, that has to be generated in the mind. Autistic children tend to struggle with pretend play; they don't think in abstract terms. And Tom was the same, a concrete thinker.

Luke would tell Tom about his plans for the business, but Tom couldn't engage, because it was just something in Luke's mind, something that might happen at some point in the future. For Tom to be interested in something, he needed it to be tangible. So, I had to be very concrete in my communications with Tom, and the same went for when he was in the gym.

There's no point shouting things at Tom before he lifts, because there'll be too much to process and it will overwhelm him. And there's no point talking in metaphors – 'reach for the stars' or 'go harder' – because metaphors are too abstract and don't mean anything to him. So, we made his instructions very short and very concrete. The first event we had success in was the Hercules hold. We advised Luke to make sure the gym was quiet before telling Tom to 'squeeze and hold'. Tom did the hold for over a minute, which he'd never done before. That's all he needed – concrete instruction, two short words.

Maybe you're thinking, 'She's this expert they've asked to help and all she's really doing is telling Tom to pick things up.' You'd be right to a certain extent, in that a lot of what I eventually advise is simple common sense. But it's about finding out what an individual needs, and working with them so they can tolerate hearing and connecting with it. Once we understood that Tom needed his instructions to be as short and clear as possible, he could focus on those words and nothing else. And once he'd got that physical feedback, had that concrete experience he could connect with, we started getting results.

In the early days, I'd advise Tom's coach Dan about the language he should use with Tom. I can remember Dan trying to explain the combination movement required for a dumbbell press and recommending that Tom imagine a triangle in his head to press through. Tom really struggled with this abstract idea generation and in the end I said to Dan, 'Just tell him to pick it up and press it.'

Such an approach doesn't always lead to the best technique. And Tom could probably improve his pressing if he nailed that combination movement – he mostly uses his arms in the dumbbell press, and barely his knees, which is incredible really. But that's just the way it has to be with Tom. If you concentrate too much on technique, he'll get anxious and won't be able to lift the weight and he'll think he'll never be able to lift it. There are no grey areas in Tom's mind. He calls himself King of the Stones, so he is the King of the Stones. And as long as he tells himself he's the world's strongest man, he will be.

Another thing Tom and I spoke about was stimulation. In autistic people, their vestibular system, which is in the inner ear and creates a sense of balance and spatial orientation, is often either under-stimulated or over-stimulated. When you see an autistic child rocking forward and back, they're over-stimulated and trying to soothe themselves. We realised that similar gentle movement would help Tom. At competitions, he'd go for short walks with Dan or Sinead to discharge a bit of energy and keep him centred.

When I started working with Luke, his sessions were all about Tom. He had to make sure Tom was okay before he could start challenging the role he'd given himself. Luke wasn't just Tom's big brother, he was his carer. That's what led him to send Tom to me. But I interpreted that as Luke saying, 'If I let someone else look after Tom, maybe I can start looking after myself.'

After I'd been working with Tom for a while, I asked if Luke could do with some help. And in the weeks leading up to World's Strongest Man in 2021, we had our first virtual session. Soon we were discussing how his relationship with Tom might be inhibiting his own performance. I'd seen YouTube videos of Luke shouting at Tom during competitions. That was Luke doing what he thought a big brother needed to do. But in doing that, he was using up so much energy, physical and emotional, and not focusing on himself. He even wanted Tom to win things rather than himself. And wanting someone else to win rather than yourself can lead to self-sabotage, albeit unconsciously.

Whenever I work with someone, I complete an assessment that informs something called a formulation, which is a visual understanding of my client and the challenges they have. With Tom, the cognitive box was much bigger than Luke's, whereas Luke's emotional box was much bigger than Tom's. That's why my specialisation in psychodynamic psychotherapy made me a good fit with Luke. Psychodynamic psychotherapy utilises the theory of psychoanalysis and ultimately how early experience shapes the conscious and unconscious world.

We identified that Luke had a caretaker role, and felt like he had to take care of and provide for everyone around him. He'd lost sight of boundaries in terms of self-care and looking after himself. He also minimised his role. He used to say he was 'just a dafty from the Highlands', suggesting his own strongman performances didn't really matter, that he didn't have big expectations.

Luke once told me that when he was posing in his budgie smugglers, covered in fake tan, he pictured me shaking my head and saying, 'Luke, what are you doing?' Some of that stuff was fine, because he was a lad who just wanted to have fun. But it suggested he still saw himself as the clown. And it reminded me that once upon a time, strongmen were circus entertainers, rather than the serious athletes most people see them as now. It was interesting that Luke connected with that aspect of strongman. And telling.

Luke and I were soon discussing his routine and how to get into the right place mentally for a competition. Tom was going to be okay, which freed Luke to go and attack, without feeling guilty that he might do better than Tom.

Because I'm a clinical psychologist, I'm interested in the whole person. So I spend a lot of time with Luke and Tom chatting about their everyday lives. I've almost become part of Tom's weekly routine, and he thinks that as long as he checks in with me everything will be alright. He knows he can speak to me about anything, in a straightforward way. If he wants to talk to me about relationships, we'll talk about relationships, because that's important to him.

I have to keep an eye on boundaries, because I don't want patients to become over-reliant on me. But more often, it's a case of making me redundant, because a patient has internalised the things we've discussed and learned to help themselves. By the time of World's Strongest Man in 2022, Luke didn't really need me. He knew what his routine should be and what he needed to do to look after himself. Suddenly, he didn't feel guilty about sitting in the corner with his headphones on, because he needed to be left alone.

Through our work together, I hope Luke, Tom and I have shown that psychoanalysis isn't scary, that it has a human face, is accessible and can be so beneficial, whether you're an elite sportsperson or not. And it's not just my patients who get something from my work – I get so much from it as well.

I'm always aware of what a privilege it is for someone to trust me with their deepest thoughts. Especially elite sportspeople, who often find speaking about that kind of stuff petrifying. I've had high-profile footballers trembling with fear on my couch, because they haven't been able to trust anyone before. And while I'd never get emotional in front of a patient, I'm certainly not a stony-faced blank slate. I'm deeply invested in my patients' wellbeing.

Psychologists should never put pressure on patients to give anything back. But Luke and Tom have given me so much, probably without even realising. To see the progress they've made since we started working together, and to see how settled and happy they are, is just wonderful. It's incredible to have played a very small part in their success – the greatest gift.

17

THE WORLD'S STRONGEST MAN

TOM

After finishing second at World's Strongest Man, I said to Dan, 'If I can add two per cent to my overall package, no-one will be able to touch me next year.' By the time the competition came around again, I'd improved by a lot more than that.

I'd trained harder than ever, maybe because my mistake the previous year had added a bit of anger into the mix. And I was just so confident of winning that it felt like a foregone conclusion. Before I even arrived in Sacramento, I went on social media and posted, 'World's Strongest Man 2021'. I'd done that before and ended up with egg on my face. But now my mind felt unbreakable, thanks to Amy.

Amy gave me a checklist for the week, so I knew exactly what to do at any given time. That was a great comfort, because I didn't have anyone else with me apart from Luke, and he had to concentrate on getting himself ready.

I thought my biggest threats in Sacramento would be defending champion Novikov and Brian Shaw. But I made it very clear to the organisers that I didn't care who was in my heat. I actually said to one of them, 'Put me in with Novikov, put me in with Brian Shaw, I'll fight anybody.'

Instead of me, Luke got drawn with Novikov in what was dubbed the group of death – and I knew Luke would go through to the finals instead of him. Even before their heat got underway, I was so sure of it. I said to Luke, 'Just be you and you'll smash that boy.' And that's what happened. Novikov finished fourth while Luke came second. He went on to win the stone-off against American Kevin Faires too, who's one of the best stone lifters in the world.

I was delighted for Luke, because there had been a lot of people writing him off. They said he was past it, that his days as a contender were over. But Luke never let all that chat – and there was a lot of it on social media – get in his head. And when Amy got involved, I could see his mindset change. From not being sure he wanted to win World's Strongest Man, he was suddenly obsessed with winning. His work in the gym went up a notch, just like mine. The harder he pushed, the harder I pushed, which had a snowball effect.

People assume hot weather would be a disadvantage for me and Luke, because of where we come from. When the temperature hits 20°C in Invergordon, people start melting. But the hotter the better as far as I'm concerned. When you train in the cold, as we often do, your muscles tend to be tighter and you're more likely to get injured. I sometimes train in jumpers, but that's not the same as heat from the sun. In contrast, when I lift things in hot countries, I find myself thinking, 'Wow, my muscles never felt so loose.'

Despite the incredible scenery, all the rain and gloom we get in the Highlands can make you a bit miserable, but when I arrived in Sacramento, which was sunny and hot, my mood and energy immediately lifted. I felt so much more alive, enjoyed my eating, kept hydrated, slept better. By the time the competition started, I'd been soaking up the sun for a week and felt like a fully charged set of solar panels.

Most of the Covid restrictions had been lifted in California, so Sacramento's waterfront was buzzing. I don't think the competition had been well promoted, because some people seemed a bit confused to see a load of gigantic blokes lifting gigantic things, but at least we had an audience.

I finished second in my heat behind American Trey Mitchell, before beating Mark Felix in a stone-off. In case you were wondering, Mark was 55 by then, still more than twice my age. Then it was back to my room, to do exactly what Amy had told me to do – which was almost nothing, except eat and sleep.

Unlike the year before, I got off to a flyer on the first day of the finals. There were no mistakes in the giant's medley, which I won by almost two seconds. Then we had to push an old steam train sitting on a wooden turntable in a full circle. The total weight was 30 tonnes, but I did it in 46 seconds, six seconds quicker than Trey Mitchell, who came in second. The frame carry, which was half of the giant's medley, and the turntable were meant to be two of my weakest events, so my confidence was now through the roof.

The third event was the keg toss, and I finished second behind Brian Shaw. That meant I led the field by five and a half points heading into day two, which was almost unheard of. That evening, people were texting me saying, 'You've done it, no-one can catch you now.' But I had to ignore all that. Yes, I remained very confident. But Brian, who was in second, was a four-time world champion for a reason. I knew that one mistake could hand him the title again, so I stayed focused.

I texted Nathan to ask what I needed to eat. I texted Dan to say, 'Good first day but still plenty of work to do tomorrow.' I didn't text Amy, which tells you everything you need to know about where my head was at. Then I got plenty of food down me and hit the hay. That night, I slept like a log for nine or ten hours.

The first event on day two was the log press, and I finished eighth out of ten. Some people probably thought that was a wobble, but that wasn't the case. I hit 185kg, and I was only hitting 180kg in training, so it was actually a pretty solid effort. Plus, I was being tactical. I was pretty sure Brian wouldn't hit more than 195kg, so I decided not to attempt a second lift, because I didn't want to hurt myself. As I'd predicted, Brian failed his third lift and finished fifth to my eighth, so I was still three points clear of him heading into the penultimate event, the deadlift.

I knew that if Brian nailed the deadlift and I slipped up, he could be ahead of me going into the Atlas Stones, the sixth and final event. Thankfully, it didn't pan out like that. I went all out and did eight reps of 350kg, which was a massive personal best. If Brian had done ten, he would have picked up three or four more points than me. As it was, he managed nine, which meant he only beat me by two points and trailed me by one overall.

This was what dreams were made of: going head-to-head with Brian Shaw, four-time winner and legend of the sport, to decide who was the greatest stone lifter and World's Strongest Man. I'd actually torn a hamstring doing the deadlift, but I wasn't going to let that affect me. By the time I'd covered my hands and arms in tacky, the sticky stuff we use for grip, I was amped.

In the production office, Brian was surrounded by his entourage, and I was all on my own. That was until Luke stormed into the room and started shouting, 'You're the best in the world!' He'd just had a bit of a nightmare in the stones, dropping one because his tacky had melted, but that's brotherly love for you. After Luke was done, I felt like I could lift a car above my head with one arm. Plus, my logical, concrete thinking had kicked in. I picked up stones all the time in training and picking up stones in a competition was no different.

The locals had come out in force for the Atlas Stones, and they didn't want to see their boy beaten. As Brian and I waited on the start line, back-to-back, all I could hear was 'U-S-A! U-S-A!' A few years earlier, all those people shouting and cheering and waving their arms around might have finished me. Now I thought, 'Let's do it ...' All I could see was the first stone, nothing else.

The whistle went and battle commenced. We were neck and neck after the first stone, but Brian had a bit of a wobble with his second and I stole a slight advantage. As he was lifting his third, I was lifting my fourth. Before attempting the fifth and final stone, I had a little look over my shoulder, to see where Brian was. I couldn't see him, so knew he wasn't on my tail. Not that I could hang around. I hauled that last stone onto my knees, straightened my legs, rolled it onto the plinth, cheered like a madman and fell to my knees. That skinny kid with autism, who people thought wouldn't amount to anything, was the world's strongest man. Sounds like a fairy tale. It was.

All those sacrifices had been worth it. The dark days in the gym, when I thought I'd rather be anywhere else in the world. All those fun nights with my mates I missed out on, doing stuff a boy in his mid-twenties should have been doing, while I was at home eating yet another plate of chicken and rice. All those photos I had to see of great occasions I wasn't part of. Not seeing my wife or dad anywhere near enough, and only seeing my nieces and nephews once or twice a month. The only thing that kept me ploughing on was the thought of being World's Strongest Man one day. And now I was.

Within seconds, Luke was giving me a big cuddle and saying, 'You've done it! You've done it!' Good job he did, because I wasn't quite sure if it had actually happened. But in hindsight, I could have done that run a hundred times and never been beaten by Brian. I'd even texted Sinead beforehand, told her I'd already won, because nobody could possibly beat me in the stones.

I felt Mum's presence that day. She was watching, no doubt about that, probably while screaming her head off and scaring all the other angels up in Heaven. More than anyone, she'd believed in me, thought I'd amount to something, when others thought I'd end up as nothing. I went through some rough times after she passed away, even wanted to quit. But I'd learned to channel that anger and darkness and become more powerful as a result.

I'd also kept the promise I made to Sinead after I quit my job. If Sinead hadn't supported my decision, I might still have been sat in that wee cabin on the building site. Sinead was the first person I called, but it wasn't much of a conversation. I was shouting, 'I've done it!' over and over again, while she was screaming. Meanwhile, her family was going mental in the background.

That was such a special moment. I'd told Sinead that me becoming World's Strongest Man would change our lives forever and now we could start putting down concrete plans. We wouldn't have anyone telling us what to do – we'd be in full control.

Dad was on a fishing trip up in Shetland, and every night he'd been crouched over his phone with a bottle of whisky, waiting for Kushi to send him the latest results. He knew I was leading going into the stones, so waiting for Kushi's final text must have been agonising. He told me that when it came through, him and his pals were cheering and hugging and weeping tears of joy. When I called him, he was blazing drunk and not making much sense. After a couple of minutes, I said, 'Jesus, Dad, I'll call you back tomorrow …'

That night was a bit of a blur. I remember going back to the hotel, getting changed, heading to a party and drinking anything that was put in my hand. And I vaguely remember speaking to the BBC, who were at Sinead's mum and dad's. All I did was shout 'I'm the World's Strongest Man!' It wasn't the greatest interview. In the end, Jordan and his film crew had to carry me back to my room. I've no idea how they did that without using a forklift truck.

· · ·

When I fell out of bed the following morning, I started to make sense of everything. I wasn't just proud that I'd won it, I was proud of how I'd won it. Unlike some of my rivals, I'd kept my head and stayed positive when things hadn't gone my way. And when Brian started coming like a train, and people thought I might crumble, I stood taller than ever. I went head-to-head with a four-time champion, a strongman legend, on his home soil and beat him. And I hadn't beaten him by one or two points, like Sinead and I had predicted – I'd beaten him by three.

I'd also done it without Sinead, Dad and my coach being there. They'd been sending me positive messages the whole time, which boosted my energy and made me feel stronger, but I didn't have their support on tap.

I won World's Strongest Man not just by performing well in the events, but because of what I did when I wasn't competing. I stuck to the script, as laid out by my team. I ate, hydrated and recovered properly. I didn't socialise, not even with Luke. Maybe Luke's support, all that shouting and hollering, made me more dominant, but I'm convinced I still would have won it without him.

On the plane home, I felt like a celebrity. People were coming up to me and saying, 'Aren't you the guy who just won World's Strongest Man?' And there was more of the same when I touched down in Scotland. Our families were waiting for us at the airport, as well as complete strangers who'd come to congratulate me. That was a cool feeling. When Sinead saw me, she ran and gave me a big cuddle. Dad was back on planet earth, but almost speechless.

What a welcome we got back in the Highlands. There were congratulation signs all along the A9, and when we arrived in Invergordon everyone was buzzing. I don't think it felt real for them either, a lad from their wee town being the strongest man in the world. It was lovely I'd made my own people so happy. And I couldn't help thinking of Opa, who'd made the Highlands his home. In his later years, Opa wrote a memoir. The final words are, 'I had survived after all.' Of course, what I'd experienced didn't compare to the horrors of war. But I had overcome my own problems. And just like Opa, I'd achieved more than anyone in their wildest dreams would have thought.

People were coming up to Dad in the street, shaking his hand and slapping him on the back, and he didn't know them from Adam. One day, he was in the supermarket in Alness and one of the checkout women gave him a big hug. She said to him, 'You don't know me, but I know you. I'm so proud of your sons!'

For weeks, I drove around with the trophy on my passenger seat, because I wanted as many people as possible to see it. It was theirs as well as mine. I broke it two or three times and had to get it fixed. It then spent some time in our gym, before I gave it to Dad. I didn't want it in my house, because I thought seeing it every day would make me less hungry. Plus, Dad deserved it for everything he'd done for me. Every time he has a visitor, he says, 'That's what Tom won for winning World's Strongest Man.' And he grins from ear to ear. I know how proud he was of his dad. And I know he's just as proud of me.

18

COMPETING WITH THE BEST

LUKE

had three or four months with Amy before World's Strongest Man 2021, and I felt like a different animal heading over to Sacramento. When people saw what heat I'd been drawn in, along with a couple of very good Americans and Oleksii Novikov, they thought I had no chance of making the finals. But I knew I'd prove them wrong.

Oleksii is a great guy and a tremendous competitor, but going up against the defending champion just got me more excited. The organisers actually suggested that I swap groups, because someone pulled out injured and things needed to be rejigged, but I refused. I relished the challenge of competing in the group of death, and thought I'd romp through.

Novikov had a bit of a shocker in the first event, the loading medley, but I think most people assumed he'd make up the ground and go through. It didn't pan out like that.

After the penultimate event, the pressing medley, I was interviewed by Eddie Hall. I came out with all the usual stuff, about how happy I was with my performance and how good I felt, but when Eddie asked if I had anything else to say, I have to admit that I got a bit emotional.

Novikov could only finish fourth in the pickaxe hold, before I beat Kevin Faires in the stone-off to make the finals. Putting out the reigning champion was a big feather in my cap, but I really thought I could finish on the podium. I knew I wouldn't score many points in the deadlift, because I rarely do. But I was confident I'd win the log press, and maybe the giant's medley, because I'm good in moving events. I knew I was unlikely to beat Tom in the Atlas Stones, unless he made a big mistake, but I still expected to take big points. I'd been dealt a good hand, which is a big part of any strongman competition.

I was fifth after three events, but smashed the log lift, hitting 215kg, 10kg more than the next man. That left me third overall. The deadlift didn't go so well, but I was still on for a podium finish going into the stones. Then disaster struck. I'm a typical sweaty Scot, which isn't great when it's 40°C. And I knew something was up with my tacky on the very first stone. It felt like a big bar of soap and kept slipping down my arms. I might as well have slathered myself with butter. I soldiered on, but each stone was a massive effort, and I wasn't able to get the last one on the plinth. I'd had a sniff of a top-three finish but now I'd tumbled down the rankings and finished seventh, again.

That was a very bitter pill to swallow, and part of me wanted to head straight back to the hotel and sulk. But while I was cleaning myself up, I thought, 'Wow! Tom's up next! He's stuck in the production office with Brian and his mob, and they'll all be whooping and hollering, like Americans do …'

I ran to the office, kicked the door open and started screaming at Tom: 'This is your time! Don't worry about anyone else!

You're the best in the world!' Meanwhile, Brian and his guys had fallen silent. They were just standing there staring at me, eyebrows raised, in disbelief. I was still screaming at Tom as he walked out of the door: 'What are you doing it for? Who are you doing it for? Come on!' I still get emotional thinking about it.

Tom's first day had been extraordinary, and almost everyone expected him to beat Brian in the final event. They didn't call him 'King of the Stones' for nothing. But there's always stuff going on behind the scenes that people don't know about. Tom says he slept well after day one of the finals, but I remember differently. He wasn't feeling the best and was sick a couple of times. That might have been nerves, or it might have been fatigue. Whatever it was, he wasn't at his best on day two. But even after he tore his hamstring doing the deadlift, I knew he'd have too much for Brian in the Atlas Stones.

Sure enough, Tom's performance was the best I'd ever seen. When he turned to see where Brian was, just before lifting the final stone, he reminded me of the wee kid I once knew. Uncertain, a little bit scared. But Brian was nowhere to be seen. Tom had held his nerve and demolished one of the greatest strongmen who's ever lived. It wasn't even close. And that scene afterwards, of me cuddling Tom and on the ground, is one of the most iconic in the history of World's Strongest Man. When I got home to Scotland, I had it tattooed on my arm, because I never want to forget it.

Jordan and his team were in Invergordon to film Sinead and Kushi's reactions. That was mostly them crying down the phone. I managed to keep my composure for a while, until one of the organisers, a girl called Becca, looked at me and her bottom lip started wobbling. That set me off as well.

As the tears flowed, Tom's life flashed before my eyes. I saw him as the frightened little boy who couldn't leave the house. I saw him as the lanky, awkward kid on his first day in the gym. I saw him at his first competition, when he was too scared to talk to anybody. I saw his tantrums when things didn't go his way. I saw his anxiety before his first international competition – the 7am phone calls, panicking about tickets and flying. I saw his first World's Strongest Man appearance in Botswana, when he injured his shoulder and had to withdraw. I saw his disastrous appearance in Britain's Strongest Man, when he finished last. I saw him lifting that final stone again, roaring and falling to the ground. It was barely believable, even when I played it all back in my head.

Then I saw Mum, who more than anyone else made the impossible possible. I thought of the hours and hours she put in, to make Tom feel safe leaving the house, going to school, playing football. I thought of her joy at Tom getting a job, getting a girlfriend, moving out, becoming a strongman. Things that can be tricky for anyone, let alone someone with autism.

I wondered how many other kids had been written off because they lacked the same unwavering support; lacked a mum who went above and beyond, instilled drive and ambition in her offspring. I wish she'd been there to see Tom become World's Strongest Man. It was such a beautiful sight.

• • •

I think it took a while for Tom to understand what he'd done. After lifting that final stone, he didn't have a moment to himself for the next few hours. First, he had to put up with me mauling him, then he had the trophy presentation, then he had his media interviews. At some point I told him I'd see him back at the hotel, where we'd get cleaned up before heading off to the party.

Tom would have gone straight to bed if Sinead hadn't told him to go out and celebrate, but I was mad for it, because I hadn't partied for months. I had a 20-second shower, got dressed, hot-footed it to the hotel bar and started sinking beers. On the bus to the party, I started a chant – 'Tom Stoltman, World's Strongest Man!' – and soon everyone had joined in. Even Brian!

The party was in a pool bar in a plush part of Sacramento. And the drinks were free. Tom started out tentatively, sticking to bottles of beer, but I got straight on the whisky. After two or three of those, I was already feeling it. Then us strongmen started mingling with the TV people, execs and all, and things got a bit out of control. As the sun was setting, I ordered a bottle of champagne.

I didn't make the bus home, but I've seen the videos. Almost all the competitors were on there, chanting Tom's name and slapping Brian on the head. It was like a coach ride home from a cup final: absolute bedlam. The party continued back at the hotel too, which was a lot of fun.

Tom woke up on the floor of his room, feeling a little bit worse for wear. And when he phoned Sinead, she was with the

BBC again. There followed a lot of crying and shouting, of the happy, delirious kind. The flight home was pretty rough, but the welcome was wonderful. Tom had to do endless media interviews, but he coped with all the attention well. He'd come a long way in so many respects.

The following weekend, we had a party for family and friends in Inverness. It was a great night, with lots more drinking and singing. At some point, I took a seat in the corner and watched the merriment, feeling dead emotional. Eventually, I said to Kushi, 'Tom doesn't have a clue what he's done. It still hasn't sunk in.'

I was looking at the trophy in his hand, thinking, 'That represents all the hard work we've put in over the last however many years. And Tom doesn't seem at all bothered.' I honestly think he was more excited that Rangers had tweeted about his win than the win itself.

I remember Colin Bryce saying to me, 'It's brilliant to see Tom just enjoying himself.' And Tom enjoyed himself a lot in the three or four months after winning World's Strongest Man. I went out with him once – that was enough for me. And I did eventually say to him, 'Come on now, maybe it's time to stop partying and start training properly again.' But he was still a lad in his twenties and deserved to enjoy his time as champion.

If you can't enjoy winning World's Strongest Man, then what's the point? He'd cemented his name in history, alongside strongman legends like Bill Kazmaier, Geoff Capes, Jón Páll Sigmarsson, Magnús Ver Magnússon, Mariusz Pudzianowski, Žydrūnas Savickas and Brian Shaw. But I don't think any of those boys would have partied for as long and as hard as Tom did. That's what I love about my wee brother – he doesn't think he's anything special, just like Opa didn't think he was anything special, despite living the life of ten men. He's just Tom, who happens to be the World's Strongest Man.

19

STRONGEST BROTHERS IN THE WORLD

TOM

I t's fair to say I went off the rails a bit after becoming World's Strongest Man. But I think I had a right to. I sacrificed a lot to win that trophy. I was still a 27-year-old boy and I'd hardly seen anyone for months, apart from Luke and my wife. And if you win World's Strongest Man and go straight back to training the following week, you're a bit weird. In fact, you're not human. So, I said to Sinead, 'I've done what I promised I was going to do, so now I'm going to take time off training, spend time with you and do whatever else I fancy doing.'

It's not like I could have done much training anyway, because of all the media commitments. I knew people would be interested in my story, because I was the first Scotsman to win World's Strongest Man and the first guy with autism. Plus, there was the brothers angle, which intrigued people. But never in a million years did I think I'd get as much attention as I did.

I did pretty much every BBC outlet – TV, radio and online – Sky, *Good Morning Britain*, local and national newspapers. After a couple of weeks, the media requests started drying up. I thought, 'Yes, it's over!' Then stuff started getting broadcast and published, other outlets saw it and things started up again.

It was stressful at times, but it served a purpose. They were big platforms, with millions of consumers, and it felt lovely that so many people wanted to hear my story.

At weekends, it was mainly football. I was invited to Rangers' pre-season training, met all the players and had my photo taken with the Premiership trophy, which they'd just won for the first time in ten years. I'd been dreaming about that sort of stuff since I was a wee boy. I'll never stop loving Rangers, and it's no exaggeration to say that without that club I wouldn't be successful at strongman. They're a distraction, a release valve, and everyone needs those.

When the new season started, I was at every game. I was sponsored by a Rangers pub called the Bristol Bar, and every time I was down in Glasgow, I'd be in there partying all night.

I did find time to hang out with my family, which was great. I went out with Dad a few times and spent time with my sisters, nieces and nephews. I also caught up with mates, which was a bit of a relief. For months before World's Strongest Man, they'd been messaging me, asking me to come out for drinks or dinner. And every time I said no, I felt rubbish.

They could easily have said – just like Sinead could easily have said – 'I don't want anything to do with you. The only person you think about is yourself.' Luckily, they were proper mates who understood my situation. And while they loved the fact I was now the strongest man in the world, they didn't treat me any different. I'd walk in the pub and someone would say, 'Jeez, it's the World's Strongest Man, how cool is that!' Then they'd start taking the piss.

For the first two or three months after winning World's Strongest Man, I was at home for two weeks in a row maybe once. And eventually I realised all that upheaval wasn't doing me any good. Because of all the travelling, I wasn't eating properly and only training once or twice a week. I couldn't make plans for me and Sinead, like a holiday or even a couple of nights away, because someone might phone me, telling me I needed to be in England instead.

When I competed in a Giants Live event at the Royal Albert Hall in London, I was only about 60 per cent fit and finished fifth, miles behind the winner Oleksii Novikov. Eventually, it all started getting too much for me. It had been a special time in so many ways, but I started worrying I'd never get back into a routine. And while it was nice meeting fans as the World's Strongest Man, I knew that people would soon forget about me if I didn't get back to winning.

Thankfully, things started to ease off in September. And just before Europe's Strongest Man, I knocked the partying on the head and got back into full-time training. Unfortunately, I ended up missing the event because of Covid. I don't think I'd have been competitive, what with all the distractions in my life. But I was gutted to miss out, because while I was isolating in Invergordon, Luke was putting in his greatest performance. But I'll let Luke tell you all about that.

A couple of weeks later, I was second behind Luke at a Giants Live event in Glasgow. And after that, it was all about Britain's Strongest Man 2021, which I still hadn't won. People must have thought I was still neglecting my training, because they kept saying Adam Bishop, the defending champion, was going to beat me. I'd do an interview and they'd say, 'Bishop's going to hit ten reps in the deadlift. What are you gonna do about that?' And I'd reply, 'He's not gonna hit ten in the deadlift. He's gonna hit eight, I'm gonna hit eight and I'll end up beating him by five points.' In the lead-up to the competition, I was telling everyone I'd win it, and I didn't care if anyone thought otherwise.

I hadn't been back in full-time training for long, but I was right to feel confident. I was second behind Luke in the first event, the dumbbell medley, and third in the yoke, which Bish won. But that was the only time I finished outside the top two all day. My team had transformed me into a machine. I'd get up on the stage for an event and have almost nothing in my head. When I was announced to the crowd, I didn't move. Then when the whistle went, I'd eat up whatever was in front of me. No thinking, just doing. The way it had to be.

Like I said would happen, I matched Bish's eight reps in the deadlift, before blitzing the loading race, which left me three points clear of Bish heading into the Atlas Stones. There was no way I was blowing it from there. I did my five stones in just under 19 seconds, two seconds ahead of the next man and over three seconds ahead of Bish, who took fourth in the event and second overall.

Afterwards, I kept thinking, 'Where the hell did that come from?' Off the back of not much training, I'd dominated a world-class field, winning by six points, instead of the five I'd predicted. I think everyone was as shellshocked as me. I was the first Scotsman to win Britain's Strongest Man for 26 years and only the second ever. Even better, Luke and I now had all the major titles sewn up – a Stoltman was the strongest man in Britain, the strongest man in Europe and the strongest man in the world. I doubt another pair of brothers will ever match that.

• • •

The subsequent TV broadcast of World's Strongest Man led to another flood of media requests. But this time I was a lot more choosy, only doing stuff I really wanted to do. It had been a whirlwind few months and I hadn't had time to properly reflect on what I'd achieved. Thankfully, my next competition, Britain's Strongest Man 2022, wasn't for another four months.

I'd never been that interested in the money side of strongman, but it was nice to be able to say to Sinead, 'We're doing okay now.' Prize money alone wasn't going to set us up for life, but the Stoltman brand might. Being World's Strongest Man gave me more power and more control. I could decide who I wanted to work with and what I was prepared to do for them. I could choose who I wanted in my team – and I had a choice of the very best. I could choose to skip those events which no longer got the juices flowing.

By winning the biggest events, I was helping the business grow bigger and bigger, which benefited everyone involved. The Stoltman brand hadn't really excited me before then. All I was interested in was winning World's Strongest Man, not sitting behind a desk in an office. And I struggled with anything that wasn't concrete. But now I started to get more involved.

I realised that we need something to fall back on when our strongman careers come to an end. And I loved watching it grow, from that tiny office in the gym to the big place we've got now, with merchandise coming out of our ears.

Plus, Stoltman HQ doubled as a den, a place where we could hang out and have fun. I hated doing the YouTube videos at first, was really uncomfortable having a camera stuck in my face. But after a while, I almost forgot it was there. I was able to act natural and wing things, and hopefully be funny and entertaining. When we started doing our podcast, I discovered I was able to chat about pretty much anything, and those podcasts can get pretty deep. Hopefully we'll persuade a few Rangers legends to come on. My dream guest would by Ally McCoist, the club's top goal-scorer who won ten league titles. Mind you, if we did get Ally on, I'd probably be too awestruck to say anything.

I'd always said to Sinead, 'I want to win World's Strongest Man for both of us', and she'd always replied, 'Win it for yourself, because you work harder than anyone else.' Luke's right, I did start winning things for myself. But I couldn't help noticing how much my victories had meant to other people.

By becoming World's Strongest Man, I'd proved so many people wrong, not just my old PE teacher. I'd also inspired thousands of autistic kids all over the world. They'd seen a guy who supposedly had something wrong with him beat a bunch of guys who were supposedly normal. That's why I started referring to my autism as my superpower, because I wanted people to know it can actually be an advantage. Whenever I posted 'Autism is my superpower' on social media, I'd get kids replying, 'Wow! I'm like Tom Stoltman, the World's Strongest Man, and I can do anything!' Instead of their autism being a negative thing, they now saw it as a positive, something to be proud of.

When I discovered the gym, I also discovered that shifting weights and autism were the perfect match. But that was only my experience. The fact is, there are loads of things autistic people are good at. Chances are, they're probably a lot better than you at something, even if they haven't discovered that something yet. They might be amazing at maths or drawing or languages. They might have memorised every Harry Potter book. Whatever their special talent is, it's a result of their autism, the superpower they share with me.

But it wasn't just autistic people who could look at me and say, 'If he can do it against all odds, why can't I?' Anyone who'd had a tough upbringing, for whatever reason, could take inspiration from my story. Poor kids from rough areas, kids with unsupportive parents, kids with other supposed disabilities. Just about any kid who'd previously believed they'd never amount to anything.

Kids often come up to me and say, 'I want to be World's Strongest Man.' And I always say to them, 'Train as hard as you can and make it happen.' But it doesn't have to be something as big as that. It might simply be joining a gym, taking up dancing or learning to play a musical instrument. Whatever it is, saying the right words to fill them with hope is the most important thing.

My message to kids is, 'Don't listen to the naysayers. Do whatever you want to do.' Put yourself in uncomfortable situations you think you can't handle, because that's the only way to overcome your fears. And if you do handle them, you'll feel on top of the world. Dream big and go out and smash it. Some dreams might not work out, like my dream of becoming a professional footballer. But if you surround yourself with positive people and have a good support network around you, other dreams will. And if that network doesn't exist at home, like it did for me, it's about pointing them in the direction of good people who want to help.

Over Christmas 2021, I was able to spend quality time with my wife and family, not worrying too much about training or watching what I ate. And I realised my story was their story, that we'd all been on a fantastic journey together. If it wasn't for my family, I might still have been that traumatised kid, too scared to talk to people or look them in the eye. If it wasn't for Sinead, I might still have lacked the confidence to deliver on my promise. It wasn't an easy journey. In fact, it was a bloody hard slog at times. But now I was proud of the person I'd become. The strongest man in the world, a successful businessman, a good son, a loving husband. And just your regular guy.

20

STOLTMAN STRENGTH AND PRIDE

LUKE

n the lead-up to Europe's Strongest Man in 2021, my mind was unbreakable. I felt like I could have walked into a hail of bullets and emerged unscathed. You could call it 'the Opa mindset'. What that man went through doesn't bear thinking about. But it didn't destroy him, it made him stronger, in mind and body. Sometimes, I'd think about that old photo of Opa carrying a huge log on his shoulder, with a big smile on his face – the personification of fortitude.

By then, training had become an almost meditative thing for me. I loved to train by myself, with no distractions whatsoever. That way, it was just me doing something I loved. I'd strive for the perfect lift. Before I did a log press, I'd be in a Zen state of mind, free of anxiety and bad feelings. As for the press itself, everything would have to be so clean. It would have to sit perfectly on my shoulders, I'd have to pop it perfectly. And if I nailed it, I'd be elated, because so much time and effort had led to that moment.

That's why people get addicted to lifting weights, because when you get it right, it's a real buzz of euphoria, the best feeling in the world. It takes me ages to come down from that high. Sometimes, I'll be up until three in the morning, buzzing. I get tingles just thinking about that feeling.

When the events for Europe's Strongest Man were announced, I really thought I could beat Tom, so I was gutted when I found out he had Covid. But then I thought, 'Tom not being there means I *have* to win this title. I need to perform, to show I'm not just a Stoltman add-on, I'm a great strongman in my own right.'

When I turned up in Leeds, I was in a world of my own. After the competition, Dan said he was terrified of saying the wrong thing to me in case I ripped his head off. When one of the organisers asked if he could speak to me for a second, I gave him short shrift. Everyone knew a different person was competing this year, a guy who wasn't focused on anything but himself.

Previous years, I was always trying to be the funny guy, playing up to the crowd and making people laugh. I was the guy who made sure other people were okay, a giver rather than a taker. Amy had noticed this, told me that people were always sucking energy from me. So, I decided that while it was good to be a nice guy in general life, it didn't work in professional sport.

When you're competing, at least in an individual sport, you shouldn't give anything to anyone. You're there to do a job to the best of your ability, not mess around. It's not a hobby. I was incredibly privileged to be doing what I was doing for a living, so it was disrespectful not to take it seriously. It sounds cheesy, and extremely American, but I needed to be the best version of me.

I was one of the favourites in Leeds, having beaten Novikov in Sacramento. Tom was laid up with Covid in Invergordon, defending champion Luke Richardson was injured, while Georgia's Konstantine Janashia, who finished just above me at World's Strongest Man, wasn't there either.

Before the competition kicked off, Jordan interviewed Colin Bryce for our documentary. When Jordan asked if I had a chance of winning it, Colin replied, 'Well, if he doesn't win it, I think his strongman career is over.' Colin's a good lad, and I think he said that for dramatic effect, but there were certainly people thinking, 'He's getting on at 35, maybe he'll call it a day if he can't win this in his brother's absence.'

I knew my battle with Novikov would go down to the wire, because he's just such a great competitor. Going out early in Sacramento would have stung his pride, and since then he'd won a competition in London and finished second in another in Manchester. But I had that same Zen state of mind I usually only felt when I was on my own in the gym striving for perfection.

The first event doubled as the World Log Lift Championships, and Oleksii and I were two of only three competitors to score points, the other seven failing at the first weight. Graham Hicks and I took joint first, before second place in the shield carry left me miles ahead at the top of the table. Graham and Oleksii both cut my lead in the deadlift, but I was back on form in the car walk. In that event, we had to carry a 450kg Beetle frame 20 metres, which I managed in 13 seconds, just behind Oleksii. Oleksii and I were like a couple of heavyweight sluggers, trading blow for blow. But neither of us was going to go down – this battle was going the full distance.

Heading into the final event, I led Oleksii by two and a half points. I knew he'd blitz the stones, but I also knew I was more than capable of finishing within two places of him, which is all I needed to do to win the trophy. It was absolutely electric in the arena – 10,000 fans sitting in the dark, the lights trained on me and Oleksii – and as soon as that whistle went, I tore into those stones. I was ahead of Oleksii after the first, second, third and fourth stone, but he picked the last one up like it was a pebble to beat me by a couple of seconds.

I couldn't celebrate like Tom had celebrated in Sacramento, because I wasn't sure where I'd finished in the stones. But when they announced the times, I knew I'd done it. I couldn't speak when the interviewer stuck his microphone under my nose. All I could do was laugh, because I was so incredibly happy. In fact, and as I said at the time, it was the happiest I'd ever felt. Then when I started to speak, the emotions started flooding out. Me and my baby brother, rulers of Europe and the world. How cool is that?

Everyone seemed very happy for me, including my fellow athletes. Oleksii, my good friend, couldn't have been more gracious. Kushi was in the arena, and for her to see me win something was perfect. All that time I'd been away from her – while I was in the gym, in the warehouse, in the office, on the road or up to my neck in freezing water – had paid off. That dream I'd sold her, which required her to often put up with me being tired, sore and grumpy, wasn't a dream at all. It had come true, and it was lovely to see her with a big smile on her wee face and tears of joy running down her cheeks.

But more than anyone else, I needed to win that competition for myself. Besides the glory of victory, I'd proved I was no longer in a muddle, putting my needs second behind Tom's. And I'd proved I was a bona fide big beast of a strongman, not just Tom's older brother. I now felt that winning World's Strongest Man wasn't some pipe dream, it was a distinct possibility.

● ● ●

Some people probably expected me to fade away after becoming Europe's Strongest Man. I'd won the second biggest event on the calendar at the age of 35 and my wee brother was expected to dominate the sport for years to come. Where would my motivation come from? But sitting in front of the fire with a rug over my legs didn't really appeal to me. Instead, I returned to Scotland, got together with my team and tried to work out how to get better. My victory in Leeds was a great day, no doubt. But I hadn't been perfect.

The rest of 2021 was busy on the strongman front, including finishing fourth at Britain's Strongest Man, and by the time I got to Texas for the Rogue Invitational, my body was in bits. Oleksii finished ahead of me in every event that weekend, which tells you how far my form had dipped in the space of a couple of months. But at no point did I think, 'I'm getting towards my late thirties, my body's creaking, maybe I *should* knock it on the head.'

Yes, age was a factor. Tom was ten years younger than me, and I had 11 years on Oleksii. But I was still young at what I did, because I'd only been a strongman for eight years. I spent a lot of time sore, but all athletes are like that. And compared to the pain Mum went through, and the terrible things Opa experienced, it was nothing. Most importantly, I still loved training and competing – and why would anyone walk away from something they loved?

Maybe if I'd stopped getting stronger, I'd have considered calling it a day. What would be the point if I was treading water and others were flying past me? But that wasn't the case. I'd overworked my body, that was all. And I knew that if the me who turned up to Europe's Strongest Man that year ever turned up to a World's Strongest Man, I'd have a very good chance of winning it. On New Year's Day 2022, Kushi wrote on a whiteboard in the house, '144 days until World's Strongest Man.' Every day that rolled by, she updated the number. That was all that mattered now.

• • •

After a four-month break from competing, I was back in action at Britain's Strongest Man in February 2022. It didn't go as planned. That's the thing about being a professional sportsperson: just when you think you've got it cracked, something happens to let you know you've still got a way to go.

I did well in the opening event, the shield carry, but my left quad went into spasm in the deadlift for reps. I thought it would calm down and I'd be able to continue. When it didn't, I got a bit panicky and decided to withdraw from the competition. I was due to fly out for the Arnold Classic a few days later and didn't want to miss a date with my old hero Schwarzenegger.

My first appearance at the Arnold Classic was a dream come true. After the log lift, which I smashed, I got a high five from Arnie and we chatted for a couple of minutes. He said to me, 'It's all in the mind and I could tell how focused you were.' I was thinking, 'Yeah, but I'm also pretty strong ...'

As you can imagine, Tom was more excited about meeting Arnie than he was about the actual competition – he loved his films as a kid, especially *Jingle All the Way* – and I don't think his heart was really in lifting things. I managed to finish third, while Tom finished down in seventh.

Like the year before, Europe's Strongest Man in Leeds was a ding-dong battle between Oleksii and me (Tom decided to skip it, partly because it didn't fit in with his training cycle, partly because he wanted to watch Rangers play Celtic). And, once again, it all came down to me against Oleksii in the Atlas Stones. I needed him to have a nightmare to retain my title. Unsurprisingly, he didn't, beating me in a photo finish. But I didn't mind. If I was going to lose to anyone, I wanted it to be Oleksii, especially with what was going on in his native Ukraine.

In May 2022, it was back over to Sacramento for World's Strongest Man. Training went great and I breezed through my group, winning three of the first four events and not having to bother with the final one. But I wasn't dealt the best hand in the finals, not least because there wasn't a log press. There was the Flintstone barbell, but that's behind the neck, and my flexibility isn't the best. And having had high hopes of making the podium, I only managed to finish seventh overall, the same as the year before.

I left California feeling like a failure. I'd now finished seventh three times, and anything less than a podium finish just wasn't good enough. But in hindsight, it was good I was so down about my performance. Had I been happy with seventh place, I'd have been finished in the sport. As it was, I was even more determined to put things right the following year.

True, I'm not getting any younger. I wake up some mornings and know things are going to hurt when I pull back the covers and step on the carpet. It might be my knee, my ankle, my shoulder or my tricep. I've got tendonitis in my patella, my lower back and my hips. That'll happen when you press dumbbells that weigh as much as beer kegs. When I'm really sore but there's a competition coming up and I can't skip training, I'll take a couple of painkillers, although I try not to do that often. Sometimes, I'm running on fumes. But that's the life of most professional athletes. As far as I'm concerned, an injury is a broken leg or a damaged bicep, not a niggly knee.

The plan is to win World's Strongest Man in 2023. If I have the perfect day, I might. But as I write, strongman is taking a backseat. Instead, I'm spending the next six or seven months with Kushi and the family, as well as concentrating on the Stoltman business. That way, I'll be hungry as hell when I start intensive training again. Ready to smash everything – and everyone.

• • •

Recently, Tom and I started doing corporate presentations. On the face of it, strongman doesn't have much in common with working behind a desk. But the fact that strongman is such an alien concept for most people is why it's so inspirational. If a couple of lads from Invergordon can get to the top in such an exotic sport, then maybe you can do that thing that seems so unattainable.

We make our talks relatable by referencing our very normal roots and the adversity we had to overcome. Strongman can teach the average person a lot about life. It's all about drive, hard work and routine. It's about committing 100 per cent to Plan A – and not having a Plan B. Because if you have a Plan B, you're more likely to give up on Plan A. It's about ignoring the naysayers, like the people who laughed when we said we'd be the strongest brothers who ever lived. It's about knowing that taking the hard route is going to be so much more rewarding in the long run. Some people are happy to tread the easy route, and that's fine. But if you want to achieve something great, something you can be proud of for the rest of your life, the hard route is the one.

It's easy to accept that something isn't going to happen for you, that you're just going to be another number on somebody's payroll for the rest of your life. But that something can happen if you put the work in. So don't make excuses and take pride in your efforts, even if they don't amount to much. Because if you don't put the work in, you'll resent it further down the line. It will chew you up, turn you into one of those bitter people down the pub, talking about what they coulda, shoulda done.

What we do proves the body and mind are capable of so much more than most people think they are. It teaches people not to fear trying apparently crazy, dangerous things. It teaches that life doesn't have to be mundane. People are often scared of doing something unusual, because they don't want to stick out like a sore thumb and risk looking stupid. But living a weird life is brilliant. I'll be in the middle of nowhere in Botswana, pulling a 15-tonne bus 25 metres, and I'll think, 'How on earth did I end up here?' Or I'll be up to my neck in water on Loch Morlich, taking in the frosted beaches and snow-capped mountains, and I'll think, 'This is an odd way to earn a living – but I love it!'

Thank God I learned that life doesn't have to be normal before it was too late; that having been stuffed in a pigeon-hole as a youngster, I didn't have to stay in there for the rest of my life, feeling cooped-up and anxious. That's not normal anyway. Normal is doing what you want to do, rather than what other people say you 'should' or 'shouldn't' do. For me, normal is being Luke Stoltman – professional strong-man and one of the strongest men on the planet. A guy who competes all over the world and owns a business. A guy who lives and dies by his own efforts, who is his own man, rather than a number.

When I'm lifting weights, I get to feel almost every emotion there is. Pain, obviously, but also ecstasy and pride, as well as disappointment and anger. I'm so lucky my job allows me to feel all those different emotions, which are absent in so many people's day-to-day lives. But I'm just doing what I think is normal – following my passion and doing what makes me feel alive.

Of course, when family is important to you, you've got even more reason to want to succeed. That's why I want to make the Stoltman name a worldwide brand, because, for me, family trumps everything. The bigger our business gets, the more comfortable Dad will be in retirement, which is what he deserves. He's one of the hardest-working people I've known and one of my biggest inspirations – Schwarzenegger's got nothing on Dad. I'll never stop believing that what Dad has achieved in life tops anything Tom and I have done.

• • •

Sometimes, I'll watch Tom training and think, 'This is wild. He's doing things no-one else in the world can do.' It's such a buzz to spend so much time next to greatness, one of the biggest thrills you can have. Tom can carry on winning World's Strongest Man for as long as he wants.

I'm not saying Tom would have been dead had he not discovered the gym. But I do dread to think what his life might have turned out like. As it is, he isn't just the World's Strongest Man, with a public profile, he's confident, a genuinely nice guy with a heart of gold. And you can't get him to shut up. I bet Mum can't believe what's gone on since she left us. I imagine her looking down on him and saying, 'How is this boy my son?' while grinning ear to ear.

As a joke, we used to tell Mum we'd be the strongest brothers in the world one day. Now it's true. And I truly believe I can win World's Strongest Man before hanging up the straps for good. It's not like Tom's going to let me beat him – and I wouldn't want him to – but he wouldn't begrudge me.

Whatever happens, I daresay the Stoltman name will be remembered for a long time to come. True, it started out as Polish, and it used to irritate Dad when we began competing and commentators and announcers kept pronouncing it wrong. But they've finally got it sussed, and now it's every bit as Scottish as MacGregor or Campbell. I'd love to see it up in lights in Invergordon, to show it's possible to do well in life, wherever you're from. And I'd love people to see the Stoltman name and equate it with strength and pride.

For hundreds of years, Scotland was synonymous with great warriors like William Wallace and Robert the Bruce. When people thought of Scotland, they thought of the clans, fiercely proud of their identity and formidable in battle. They thought of men lifting giant stones to prove their strength. They thought of Highland games – porridge-eating men tossing cabers and bales of straw. More recently, they thought of tough blokes working in shipyards or on the land, like our granddad. But sometimes, Scotland seems to be more known for the wrong things nowadays: drug addiction, alcoholism and deep-fried Mars bars.

That saddens me, because besides being one of the most beautiful places in the world, Scotland is jam-packed with

STOLTMAN STRENGTH AND PRIDE

promise. And I know that any fellow Scot who taps into that Stoltman strength and pride will succeed in life. Like Tom and me, when we do battle with the strongest men in the world, they'll feel like a Highland warrior of old.

21

ON TOP OF THE WORLD

TOM

didn't train as much as I could have done for Britain's Strongest Man in February 2022 and I didn't feel great beforehand. But I still won four of the five events in Sheffield and finished 12 points ahead of the field. It was pretty straightforward, really. And it needed to be. If I was winning Britain's Strongest Man by a point or two, I wouldn't be fulfilling my potential. I had to dominate, as well as putting on a show for the fans.

Even when you're the reigning world champion, you always have to tell yourself you're not good enough. By never being entirely happy in the gym, by thinking I'm still too weak, I'm always getting stronger. It's not like other sports where you get to the top and think there's nothing else to be done. As a strongman, you're obsessed with progression. You get a buzz from your body looking different every day. You get a buzz from lifting even one kilo more than you did the week before.

Even before I started my training camp for World's Strongest Man, I felt stronger than ever. A couple of weeks into it, my body was doing unbelievable things. It wasn't easy, because I was still having to put the work in. But unlike the year before, I didn't have to deal with Covid, so Sinead was permanently by my side, organising every aspect of my life. She wrote 'Tom Stoltman – World's Strongest Man' on our noticeboard at home and made me repeat it ten times a day. She even drew pictures of me standing on top of the podium. Unlike the year before, I didn't say I was going to win World's Strongest Man on social media. But I did tell Sinead and Dan. In fact, I told them I was going to dominate the field and win it by a distance.

Boarding the plane, I felt very relaxed. And my mind felt so powerful. As well as Sinead, Luke and Kushi, my coach Dan and the documentary crew were with me, and I imagined we were all going on a training camp together.

When I arrived in Sacramento, I felt right at home. I knew where everything was in the hotel and Sinead would have all my meals ready for me, bang on time. For the first couple of days, I chilled by the pool with the other strongmen. But after that, I wanted to replicate life at home, which mainly meant spending time with Sinead. We'd eat together, go for nice walks together, just like in Invergordon.

I didn't want to use up too much energy in qualifying, so treated it like training. Dan would knock on my door every morning, tell me to get up and pack my bag for me. He was like a dad with a lazy teenage son. I'd be asleep on the bus, while everyone else was bouncing up and down or getting themselves in the zone. I'd wake up and think, 'This is stupid, they'll be done after a few events.'

Over a five-day competition, you have to channel your aggression, otherwise you'll burn out in no time. But my rivals were all smacking themselves on the head and getting riled up before an event. I'd be thinking, 'Why were you getting all hyped up? I know you don't do that in training. And why the heck are you on the ground now, looking like you've just run a marathon?' In contrast, I visualised what I needed to do, did it and walked off, showing no emotion, just like in training. Then I'd head back to the hotel and spend the next few hours with Sinead.

I won the first four events, and only did the fifth because I had to. I lifted what looked like a 500lb cannonball for a couple of seconds before dropping it and walking off. For the first time, I didn't have to compete in the stone-off, so had 36 hours to get myself ready for the finals. The following day, I floated around in the hotel pool, not even thinking about the competition.

Martins Licis had won his last two competitions before Sacramento, and breezed through his heat, but I expected Novikov to be my biggest threat. He finished third to my second in the opening event of the finals, the giant's medley, but was dying afterwards. He won the next event, the deadlift, before setting a new world record of 246kg in the Flintstone barbell. That meant he led me by one and a half points heading into the last day – but the scoreboard didn't tell the full story.

I could see how shattered Novikov was after day one – and it wasn't just the events that were killing him. His coach was so intense, psyching him up when he should have been telling him to calm down. Meanwhile, I was getting stronger as the competition went on, as had been the plan. If you train yourself to think about nothing but lifting whatever is in front of you, without all the roaring and shouting, you'll be far less likely to overheat and burn out. That evening, I felt like there was a lot more to come. And I slept like a baby.

I knew Novikov would struggle with the penultimate event, the power stairs, which involves carrying massive things up a set of steps. Novikov's only 6ft 1in, and those steps were very high. Sure enough, after winning the bus pull, Novikov came seventh in the power stairs. And he was in pieces afterwards, physically and mentally. Meanwhile, I finished second, meaning I led him by one and a half points heading into the Atlas Stones. I knew that if I didn't make any major mistakes, I'd win it easy.

Standing on the stage, I felt supremely confident. I was the King of the Stones, so of course I was going to win. And when the whistle went, I'd already seen myself win it hundreds of times. I went through those stones like anything, completing all five in just under 26 seconds. Novikov only managed four and finished last. That meant I'd beaten him and Licis by ten and a half points.

I was the first man to defend the title since Brian Shaw in 2016, the tenth multiple champion, and only the second Briton, after Geoff Capes, to win it twice. And you know what? The second one felt sweeter than the first, because Sinead was there to see it and able to feel what I felt.

The following day was my birthday, so Sinead bought me a cake and we had a few drinks. But a couple of days after arriving home, I was back in the gym. I felt fresh as a daisy, like I hadn't really done anything. I found myself thinking, 'I could win World's Strongest Man ten times, if I really wanted to.'

• • •

In 2021, the year I won my first World's Strongest Man and Luke became the strongest man in Europe, Invergordon council put the Stoltman name on the town's welcome signs. Who'd have thought it – the strongest brothers on the planet, from a small town in the Highlands. They only mention me and Luke, but those signs are also a tribute to Opa. Luke and I are proud of what we've achieved, and incredibly appreciative of everyone who has supported us along the way. But Opa brought the Stoltman name to Scotland, and everything we've done stems from him. We're so proud to be bringing the Stoltman name to a wider audience. Hopefully, it will get to the stage that when someone mentions strongman, they'll immediately think Stoltman.

Invergordon is a small place in the grand scheme of things – we often refer to it as 'the arse end of nowhere' – but it's got some of the best people. Everyone seems proud of us and similarly, we're proud to call the town home.

But it's not as if we feel special. You can always rely on some lovely old lady to say, 'I remember you when you were a wee boy. You weren't so strong in those days.' That sort of stuff keeps you grounded. And it doesn't matter what job you do in Invergordon, everyone is part of the community and everyone supports each other.

Usually, it's the UK's big cities that produce star athletes – places like London, Edinburgh and Manchester. Only once in a blue moon does a wee place like Invergordon produce athletes like me and Luke. And that makes me feel so proud. That's one of the reasons I want to tell my story, to show that big things can happen in small places. To show that when life looks bleak and lacking in opportunities, there is always a light at the end of the tunnel, even if you can't see it and have to be led there by the hand.

Of course, the person who led me by the hand was Luke. Without him, I probably wouldn't have discovered the gym, and I probably wouldn't be a strongman. He's been such a massive part of my life and I owe him so much.

We're obviously competitive, but we've never stopped being brothers. We train together, travel the world together, run a business together, holiday together. I've learned so much from him; he's learned so much from me. When I'm competing, Luke will be screaming his head off. When he's competing, I'll be doing the same. If we're competing directly against each other, we'll both go hell for leather, before giving each other a big hug, whoever's won. When I make a mistake, he's there for me. When he makes a mistake, I'm there for him. We're strong individually, but we're so much stronger together. I guarantee there'll be a Stoltman one-two at World's Strongest Man in the next few years. And I'm confident Luke will win it before he hangs up his straps.

Luke and I are so close, people think we live together, like Bert and Ernie from Sesame Street. On social media, people are always asking me where Luke is, and I usually tell them he's probably with his wife. But it doesn't bother me. It's nice that people can see how strong our bond is.

And it's not just me and Luke – the whole Stoltman family are involved. Harry's going to be a solid strongman in a few years, and our sisters also like to watch us compete, along with our nieces and nephews. Then, of course, there's Dad, who's been through a hell of a lot, what with my autism and Mum's passing. But I know how happy it makes him, to watch me and Luke on the TV, competing in some far-off country, and to hear the commentator mention Invergordon and the Stoltman name. Dad always says my story is like something out of a comic book, almost as remarkable as Opa's.

It's a cool feeling, knowing we're among the many successful people the Highlands has produced, and in a way, we've helped to make Invergordon a more special place. Cafés and shops have people popping in, asking where they can find the Stoltmans, and our gym is now a tourist spot. We get four or five visitors every week, from all over the UK. One day, I got chatting to a guy from Kent. I said to him, 'Which airport did you fly into?' And he replied, 'I didn't fly, I drove up.' It had taken him 12 hours to get there. Another time, some guy pulled up in a camper van. When he got out, he had a guitar over his shoulder. I asked him if he was lost, and he replied, 'No, dude. I came to see the world's strongest man – can I play you a song?' I wondered if someone had spiked my protein shake and I was hallucinating. But sure enough, he played his song, before shaking my hand, jumping back in his van and saying farewell.

It blows my mind to think that people want to come all the way to Invergordon to see us, or at least the town we came from, or the gym we train in. It suggests strongman is more popular than ever, at least in the UK.

Ten years ago, Giants Live competitions took place in small halls, and they often failed to sell out. Now, they're filling 10,000-capacity arenas. I'll look out at the crowd and see elderly ladies and kids as young as five. And whenever we post on YouTube, we'll get messages from people saying they got hooked on the sport because of our videos. That's what people want nowadays, to be able to see what their heroes get up to behind the scenes.

My success in strongman has opened so many doors for me. Not so long ago, someone phoned me up and asked if I wanted to appear in a music video for the band Travis. I'd never heard of Travis, despite them being Scottish. But they flew me, Mark Felix and Rob Frampton over to Berlin and we had a great weekend. I was also invited to appear in the TV series *Gangs of London*, but I had to turn that down, because it clashed with a competition. But filmmakers are always looking for massive blokes like me, and I reckon I could do what Thor Björnsson does, playing giants and ogres in fantasy dramas.

Just before I flew out to World's Strongest Man in 2022, I was asked if I wanted to play in Soccer Aid at London Stadium later that year. Of course I did! That was actually an extra motivation in Sacramento, because I wanted to be billed as the reigning world's strongest man, not the former world's strongest man.

Soccer Aid was one of the best things I've ever done, even better than winning World's Strongest Man. I spent three days training with proper football legends, like Roberto Carlos,

Cafu and Andriy Shevchenko. Usain Bolt was our skipper, so we had the world's fastest and strongest men in our team.

They wanted me to play in goal, so I took training very seriously, because I didn't want to let loads of goals in and look like a muppet. As it turned out, the game came down to penalties, I saved one and Lee Mack scored the winner for us. Not a sentence I thought I'd ever write.

The celebrations were surreal – me jumping up and down with Usain Bolt, Lee Mack, Martin Compston from *Line of Duty*, Mark Strong from the *Kingsman* movies and all these legendary footballers. Since that night, I've had people come up to me in the street and say, 'You're that goalkeeper off Soccer Aid.' That's fine with me.

Strongman is taking a back seat until World's Strongest Man in 2023. You might have noticed I was carrying less weight at Soccer Aid. In fact, I was the lightest I'd been for years. That's because Sinead and I are trying for a baby, and I want to be as healthy as possible. Sinead has sacrificed almost ten years of her life for me, so it's time to put her first for once.

It's almost impossible to overpraise Sinead. When I first met her, I said, 'If you go out with me, you're going out with a strongman. You don't have a choice, because that's what I do.' She thought it was just talk, that I was just a meathead getting carried away with himself. Then when she saw me compete for the first time, and I dropped a log on my face and chipped a tooth, she tried to persuade me never to compete again. But she kept the faith.

Sinead was very close to my mum. She accompanied her to every strongman competition and was with her almost every day after she was diagnosed with cancer. They spoke about stuff Sinead has kept secret from me to this day. Mum spoke so highly of Sinead and was so happy I'd found her. More than anyone, Mum understood how Sinead had changed my life.

When Mum was dying, Sinead knew what I was going through and shared my pain. And when Mum passed, Sinead became a replacement parent in a way, as well as my wife. Looking after me is hard work. She is incredible 24 hours a day – she arranges my diary, tries to make sure I don't get stressed during training, keeps me calm during competitions. Similarly, I like to know if she's feeling okay or not. When she's down, I try my best to bring her up. I like to be stupid, which is important in any relationship. We still have some very good playfights, and Sinead even wins some of them. But while I'm sure Sinead would thrive without me, I'd fall apart without her. That's why I'm so determined to succeed, because that's my way of paying her back, of making her proud. If anything bad happened to Sinead, God forbid, I'd quit strongman in a heartbeat to look after her. I've always been a family man first, and Sinead has been my priority since the day we met.

I don't know how things are going to pan out, but I'd love to have a couple of kids and for them to see me win World's Strongest Man. Hopefully, I'll then be able to walk off into the sunset having won six world titles, which would make me the greatest strongman of all time.

I still love the sport with all my heart, I still love pushing my body to its limits, and I still get an enormous buzz from doing something few other humans on the planet can do. But if I don't win six world titles, or even four or five, I won't be downhearted. The vast majority of strongmen never win it, and winning it more than once puts me in very illustrious company. Maybe I'll get injured, maybe I will fall out of love with strongman one day. But if that does happen, I'll have a thriving business to fall back on. I'll still have the best wife in the world. And hopefully I'll have a couple of beautiful kids to focus on instead.

And what a story I'll be able to tell those kids. I'll describe the confused little kid I was, too afraid to leave his house or look people in the eye. The teenager written off by some as a no-hoper. The young man people thought would live with his parents forever and always have a dead-end job. But I'll also tell them how supportive Mum and Dad were. I'll tell them about the day Luke took me down the gym. How I didn't quit, despite my discomfort. How I stuck it out for once, discovered I had a passion for it, as well as a talent.

Gyms can be intimidating places for anyone, let alone a kid with autism. All those mirrors, all those eyes on you. But with Luke by my side, I gritted my teeth and got through it. Then when Luke had to go away, the gym no longer seemed like a big, bad world. I didn't feel like a scared wee baby, wanting to run away and cry. I felt comfortable. I felt confident. I felt completely at home. I felt like a common-or-garden-variety bloke, just another normal member of society.

The gym gave me all the tools I needed to thrive in life. It taught me the value of hard graft, of forcing myself to do things I didn't really want to. It improved my self-esteem and social skills. It made me realise I was as good as anyone else. It meant I could communicate with people who were supposed to be more important than me. It meant that when someone stuck a camera in my face and a microphone up my nose, I didn't feel like running away, I was quite happy to answer their questions. And it enabled me to talk to the opposite sex, which is how I met Sinead and moved out of my parents' house.

But that doesn't mean the first few years of strongman were easy. There were plenty of tough times along the way. I often took one step forwards and two steps back. And I felt like walking away a few times. Without Sinead, I might have done. That's another lesson I learned: if you want to be successful, you can't do everything yourself. At the same time, I eventually realised I had to focus on myself and not care what anyone else thought.

Sometimes I feel like pinching myself. How could a guy with autism achieve all this? But then I think it makes perfect sense. If I'd been a 'normal' guy, I probably would have finished school, gone to university and got a normal job. My autism controlled me for a long time, but it meant I didn't end up doing what most people do. I didn't end up working in an office or a factory. Instead, I went in a different direction. And once I'd got to grips with my autism, I was able to do something remarkable with my life. Now I think that being born autistic is the best thing that's ever happened to me.

That's what I'm most proud of – showing that an apparent disability can actually be your superpower. That you can grow up fragile and become robust, in mind and body. That a scared wee, autistic boy can become the strongest man on the planet. I made it, Mum. I'm on top of the world.

Afterword

LUKE

There hasn't been much strongman for me of late. After World's Strongest Man in 2022, my only other event that year was the Shaw Classic, and I withdrew after two events. Some people probably thought I'd slipped into retirement without bothering to tell anyone. Truth is, I was just taking a well-earned rest.

When I finally re-emerged, at the Arnold Classic in March 2023, I looked every bit my 38 years and finished last. The winner, Canadian Mitch Hooper, was 11 years younger and had been on the circuit for less than a year.

There were only seven weeks until World's Strongest Man, and a lot of people were writing me off. I know they're keyboard warriors, and I shouldn't let them get to me, but sometimes they mess with my mind. Thankfully, having a point to prove, not just to the naysayers, but also to yourself, can be a powerful driver. After a few days' training, I was hungry as hell.

I knew we had to make changes, and that if Tom was going to win a third world title, I had to be the older brother and lead by example.

Tom had only competed once since winning World's Strongest Man in 2022, when he finished sixth at the Arnold

Classic, although it didn't take him long to fly past me and reach another planet. After the five-week training camp, I felt stronger than I'd ever done heading into a World Strongest Man and the doubts were mostly extinguished. My body felt almost broken, but I loved how much pain I was in. That meant preparation was going well. I believed I deserved to be there and that I was going to make the final. I thought top five was possible, but my ego craved a podium place. Meanwhile, Big Tommy was looking every bit the reigning champion he was.

Myrtle Beach, South Carolina, wasn't as hot and humid as Sacramento had been two years previously. But it was still very different to Invergordon. None of the groups was easy, but I finished second behind Oleksii Novikov, before beating my good mate, the Welsh hero Gavin Bilton, in the stone-off to qualify for the final. You could see from my celebration how pumped and proud I was.

Having been lovely all week, there was rain on day one of the final. When I got to the venue, I felt a bit groggy, maybe because my adrenaline had dropped after a day's rest. As a result, I was quite sluggish in the first event, the shield carry, and only managed two reps in the deadlift. Eighth place in the Fingal's fingers meant I was languishing near the bottom of the standings.

But I woke up on day two with a lot more energy, thanks to an early night. I also felt belligerent, which pleased me. A big part of being a successful athlete is not letting bad days get to you, because they're unavoidable.

The final's fourth event was the max dumbbell, which got a bit controversial. There was a lot of online chat about lockout decisions, while athletes kept questioning the referee, which I'm not a big fan of. Then again, it showed how much it meant to everyone and was probably fun to watch.

Tom and I beat Eddie Hall's British dumbbell press record, which neither of us thought was going to happen. And having hit 132kg, I thought I'd locked out 140kg, only to be given a no rep. But I wasn't the only athlete to get an iffy decision, and getting so close gave me a huge injection of confidence.

There was more controversy in the bus pull. Six of us finished on 32 seconds, but I'm not sure how accurate the timing was. And if the course had been longer and the bus heavier, that would have created more separation.

As it was, I finished seventh, just 0.56 seconds behind Tom who came second. Mitch Hooper won, which meant he led Tom by five and a half points heading into the final event, the Atlas stones. Tom's pretty good at lifting those, but he would have needed Mitch to have a complete meltdown in order to retain his title.

The stones were surreal, because I was up against Brian Shaw, who was competing in his final World's Strongest Man. Neither of us managed to lift them all, but I was still buzzing. That's a moment I'll carry with me forever.

I finished eighth overall, which proved I wasn't washed up like some people thought. Will I break Brian's record of 16 World's Strongest Man appearances in a row? Unlikely, but I reckon I've got a few more decent years in me yet.

As for Tom, he did all he could, but it wasn't enough to topple Mitch. Still, I was so proud of my little brother. After watching him at the Arnold Classic, people doubted he'd even make the final. Instead, he finished second, his fourth podium in a row, on just a few weeks' training. And he was as gracious in defeat as he'd been magnanimous in victory the previous two years.

Can we be better prepared next time? Of course. That's the exciting thing. Mitch is an exceptional talent, but I hope he enjoys his year of being World's Strongest Man, because the Stoltmans are coming for him in 2024.

TOM

Ten months is a long time in strongman, and that's how long I was away for between winning my second World's Strongest Man and my comeback at the Arnold Classic in 2023. And while I had my feet up, a new threat emerged.

Mitch first appeared on my radar in 2022, when he qualified for the final ahead of Brian Shaw. He then reeled off seven podium finishes before his victory at the Arnold Classic, in which I finished sixth. People were saying I'd lost my hunger, that I had no chance of retaining my world title the following month, that there was a new sheriff in town. Blah blah blah. But the next five weeks went better than ever. I hit all my targets and felt confident on every single lift, which is not normally the case. By the time we left for America, I was in unbelievable shape and confident I was going to be a three-time world champion. I was convinced that the only thing that could beat me was death.

Before the competition started, I gave a big talk with some kids on the spectrum and who have additional needs. And telling all those kids that autism was my super power, and seeing their reaction, got me really fired up for battle.

I qualified for the final behind Europe's Strongest Man Pavlo Kordiyaka. That worked out nicely, because after beating Bobby Thompson in the stone-off, I knew what tacky to use in the final.

The day off was difficult, because I kept seizing up. I had physio and managed to get a good sleep, but after I arrived at the venue for 6.30am, the heavens opened and we had to hang around for four hours. When we finally got underway, Mitch beat me by a metre in the first event, the shield carry. People were saying I'd dropped it too early – and maybe thrown away the title – because I'd got complacent and thought I'd won. But I could have carried it a few more metres, used up more energy, and he still might have beaten me.

I was worried about the deadlift, especially after my poor performance at the Arnold Classic, but I did six reps of 353kg in the rain, which I was happy with. I'd only done Fingal's fingers once before, in my first World's Strongest Man, where I only made it to the second finger. But this time I went at them in an aggressive but measured way and finished first, well ahead of Mitch.

I'd lost a lot of sleep over the dumbbell event during my preparation and thought it might even cost me a place on the podium. When I failed my first attempt, I feared the worst. But I screwed my head back on and set a new British record, along with Luke. That was a special moment, because the dumbbells had been my Achilles heel for so long and I'd been telling everyone how hard I'd been working on improving. Unfortunately for me, Mitch hit 140kg for the win, and ultimately, I knew it was mission impossible from that point on.

Luke is right, the bus pull was far too light for World's Strongest Man. Apparently it was heavier than 2022, but it felt like pulling Luke's pickup. Maybe if it had been heavier, and the course longer, I'd have had a chance of beating Mitch. As it was, he finished first and I came second, which meant I was trailing him by five and a half points heading into the Atlas stones. I managed to beat him in my signature event, but it was Mitch who took the title.

Obviously I was disappointed to lose my crown, but I was philosophical about it. Considering how much time I'd had off, and the shape I was in at the Arnold Classic, finishing second was a minor miracle.

I was most proud of the fact I'd kept my head. When I started falling behind, there was part of me thinking, 'What's the point?' And the old me would have quit. But then I thought, 'Let's make a statement. If your all isn't good enough, that's fine. But let's show how much character you've got.'

I've realised it's pretty much impossible to win World's Strongest Man five or six years in a row, because anything can happen in a strength sport. As it is, four podium finishes on the spin is an incredible achievement.

Brian Shaw didn't win his first world title until he was 30, and he ended up winning it four times. I'm still only 28, so if I carry on for another ten years, I could win it six times in total, which would make me a very happy man.

I can't be having ten months off again, and I've rethought my scheduling. Only caring about World's Strongest Man doesn't work, because not only do you need to keep your body conditioned, you also need to maintain a competitive mindset, as it's not easy to turn that off and on again.

So I'll be staying busy from now on, and every competition I enter, I'll be focused, aggressive and determined to win. I tip my hat to Mitch Hooper, he's a great competitor and certainly no flash in the pan. But I'm going nowhere.